COLLEGE BOUND

AND

GAGGED

COLLEGE BOUND

AND

GAGGED

How to Help Your Kid Get into a Great College without Losing Your Savings, Your Relationship, or Your Mind

NANCY BERK, PH.D.

NANCY BERK MEDIA, LLC
PITTSBURGH

Published by Nancy Berk Media, LLC
Pittsburgh
www.nancyberkmedia.com

Cover design and illustrations by Cori Huang

Interior design, composition, and editing by Mindy Hoffbauer
for Write Angle Consulting, Inc.

Set in Times New Roman, Trebuchet MS, Octin Sports, and College Outline

Author photo by Ed Berisha for eb studio

ISBN: 978-0615548838

Printed in the United States of America

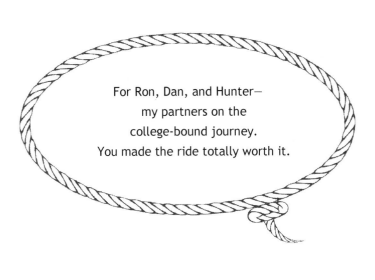

For Ron, Dan, and Hunter—
my partners on the
college-bound journey.
You made the ride totally worth it.

ACKNOWLEDGEMENTS

Many thanks to the parents, teens, and experts who shared their time and stories to help me examine every crazy detour and roadblock on the way to college.

A special thank you to my wonderful family and friends who endured hours upon hours of college chatter.

And a huge thank you to Mary Lou, Betsy, Roberta, and Kelly for their endless reviews and enthusiasm.

I am especially grateful for the extraordinary talent of Cori Huang, whose illustrations and cover design captured exactly what I had hoped, and my amazing editor, Mindy Hoffbauer, who totally understood my vision.

CONTENTS

Introduction 1

1: What to Expect When You're Expecting College 3

2: Standardized Anxiety 25

3: You're Grounded 47

4: Search and Seizure 73

5: Apply Yourself 109

6: Getting In and Checking Out 125

7: Cheers and Tears 139

Epilogue: Contradictions 155

Appendix A: College-Bound Pet Peeves 159

Appendix B: Ten Money-Saving Tips 161

Appendix C: College-Bound Favorites 163

College-Bound Shout-Out 167

About the Author 169

INTRODUCTION

Is your parental anxiety climbing as your child gets closer to college? Are you sweating the SAT® more than your kid? Do you fear a teen's college selections might be based on a great cheese steak and hot campus tour guide? This year, over three million students will graduate from high school. Approximately 70 percent will enroll in college. And at least a few million parents will tear their hair out. Stuck in a confusing, competitive, and costly process with a moody teen, parents are left searching for support, solutions, and reassurance that their kid will get into college and their family will return to normal.

When my older son began his college search, I was shocked to discover that, even as a clinical psychologist and a former admissions committee member, I was as panicked as the rest of the frantic parent pack. By the time my younger son joined the party, it was clear to me that parents needed strategy AND humor to keep smiling through the process. That's why I wrote *College Bound and Gagged*.

If you need the inside scoop on how to get the job done, but don't have time for 300 pages of dry facts, or you're searching for a little comic relief when it seems like there's nothing to laugh about, you're in the right place. *College Bound and Gagged* is the straight-talking survival guide for anyone who needs to rein in their high school student or the crazy process.

Whether it's time to buckle down or calm down, this book will give you the tips and insight you need to nurture student success, preserve family resources, and maximize relationships. *College Bound and Gagged* tackles procrastination, confusing procedures, competitive parents, standardized test anxiety (especially yours!), campus tour trauma, admissions office disasters, and all the other bumps on the road to higher education. With tips from leading college experts, top-five lists to keep you informed, helpful online and print resources, fun illustrations, and humor that will hit home, this book is the prescription for every family on the college journey.

Happy Trails!
Nancy Berk, Ph.D.

1: WHAT TO EXPECT WHEN YOU'RE EXPECTING COLLEGE

Time flies when you're a parent. One minute you're cutting crusts off grilled cheese sandwiches, and the next you're cutting college checks. And while the journey of parenthood provides you with plenty of skills and ammunition to tackle life's challenges, the college-bound experience can throw you for a loop. I thought I had the whole parent thing figured out. Then my older son applied to college and I learned there was another process as challenging as childbirth. And guess what? It also involved testing, mood changes, a little nausea and anxiety, pushing, and plenty of people weighing in on what you should be doing.

College search and selection should always be a student-driven process, but parents need to know what to expect in order to be supportive. They also need to know their family isn't the only one drowning in a sea of information and indecision. We're all in the same boat trying to navigate our teens toward happy and successful futures. Some waters are rockier than others, and it can get frustrating. Some parents become overly involved. Others get involved too late. And some just jump ship.

5 College-Bound Reminders

1. Conflict is common and normal
2. There are many wonderful schools for your child
3. You may be paying for it, but you aren't going to college
4. Money can't buy college happiness
5. One day, you will forget the pain

As a parent, you need to be an educator (not a ghost-writer, college co-ed, or overbearing stage parent). You need to keep your own agenda in check and guide your teen when necessary. You don't need a boatload of cash, a Ph.D., or college experience to be an advisor and advocate. You can be helpful without crossing the line or annoying your child. Okay, at some point you will annoy. But you can help without losing your sanity or compromising educational ethics and your child's success. You've just got to be armed with a little information and a sense of humor. Here goes....

Your Baby and You

Warning: Teens don't think like us. The sooner you realize this, the better off you will be. Teen "logic" isn't logical to an adult. Follow the "Teen Train of Thought" (Figure 1, page 23) for a little insight into the unique thought processes of the college-bound kid.

Parents of teens realize their children have inside (home) and outside (everywhere else) personalities. This is usually discovered by accident after teachers or other parents compliment your child-rearing skills. You gladly take credit, feeling fortunate that at least your kid can hold it together in public. It would be nice to have it both ways, but it would be a lot worse if children were pleasant and obliging at home only to transition into belligerent behavior when they hit the real world. Let's face it—giving grief or dirty looks to people who hand out grades, diplomas, and acceptance letters isn't recommended.

Teen attitudes can become more extreme during the college search. Whether it's adolescent egocentrism ("the world revolves around me" and "everyone's looking at me"), struggles for independence, academic obligations, application demands, or fear of the unknown, it's unpleasant and usually unavoidable. Many parents run a tight ship, but parents of college-bound teens can feel like they're running a battle ship. Some days, your world will feel like a remake of *Ferris Bueller's Day Off.* You're on guard, issuing ultimatums and always the bad guy. Life is totally repetitive. You remind, nag, go to sleep, wake up,

> Many parents run a tight ship, but parents of college-bound teens can feel like they're running a battle ship.

and do it again. You wonder how your teen will complete four years of college when she can't scare up the enthusiasm to even finish the application. You're exhausted and she probably is too.

5 Things That'll Drive You Crazy

1. The "Are You Kidding Me?" Teen Eye Roll
2. The "You NEVER Said That" Teen Hearing Problem
3. The "This Is Ridiculous" Teen Stomp Off
4. The "OMG I Can't Even Believe You" Teen Sigh
5. The "I'd Say 'I Hate You,' But I Know Better" Teen Grunt

Sarcasm

If your family had an island reality show, it's a good bet your college-bound kid would be the first one voted off. Just because your child can hurl an insult and strike any moving target (including you) doesn't mean she won't grow up to be a wonderful member of society and your family. Hold your ground and demand respect, but cut her a few breaks. You've heard of Bridezilla? This is Collegezilla and there are no gender boundaries.

Silence

Don't worry. Just when you think the sarcasm will kill you, you get the silent treatment.

Drama

And the Oscar goes to ... the drama queen and king. Silence is golden—and gone—when drama royalty hit the stage. In the spectrum of meltdowns, these exaggerated outbursts can be the most uncomfortable and, fortunately, the most fleeting. Simple challenges can bring end-of-the-world theatrics that don't respond to parent support or logic. Tread lightly. Speak softly and carefully, because one misstatement is like kerosene to the smoldering teen temper.

Procrastination

I was going to give procrastination its own chapter, but it was too depressing. Still, guidance counselors identify procrastination as the most common applicant problem. It can wreak havoc during this deadline-driven process and interfere with recommendation letters and potential financial aid options. Some counselors estimate that approximately 70% of kids need an "incentive plan" or push as they go through this process. Congratulations! Once again, as uncomfortable as it may be, your child's procrastination is probably normal.

> Batten down the hatches, choose your battles wisely, and try like crazy to be supportive.

Before you yell, remember that procrastination is genetic. Actually, I don't know that for sure, but I'd bet on it. Pretty much everything is. So, it's a little hypocritical to scream at your procrastinating senior if you were always the last parent signing your kid up for intramurals. On the other hand, it may be that the procrastinating teen isn't so much a procrastinator as more laid back than the Type A do-it-right-away kind of parent. That can be a good thing, but it will not feel like it during the high-pressured countdown to college deadlines. For those with a self-motivated, organized, deadline-respecting child, do everyone a favor. Thank a higher power that you have been spared the anxiety and then keep your mouth shut unless you are questioned. Fellow parents of the other type teens do not want to hear about how your child color-coded her applications and created an Excel® spreadsheet that she shared with you during your weekly parent-child meetings. They are frustrated and tired and have no time to find joy in their hearts for your good fortune. They are overwhelmed trying to inspire an essay. Don't jinx yourself—the chances are good that your next child will be just like theirs, so save this book!

Confusion

Confusion is normal. College applications and admissions have changed over the last few decades. So whether you've had a college experience or not, there's lots to learn.

It doesn't help that nothing's spelled out and everything's an acronym. AP®. ACT®. SAT. GPA. ED. EA. Each one seems more important than the next, and by the time you figure out what a FAFSA is, you need an EKG and a bodyguard for your IRA. Below is a handy definition list that will keep you on your toes. I've also provided my alternative definitions to help you prepare. I'm exaggerating, but that's what exasperated parents do.

College-Bound Acronyms

Acronym	Real Definition	Exasperated Parent Definition
ACT	American College Test	Another Challenging Task
AP	Advanced Placement	Accelerated Panic
EA	Early Action	Earlier "Attitude"
ED	Early Decision	Earlier Drama
FAFSA	Free Application for Federal Student Aid	Futile Attempt for Securing Assistance
GPA	Grade Point Average	Getting Pretty Anxious
PSAT®	Preliminary SAT	Preliminary Situational Anxiety Test
SAT	Scholastic Assessment Test*	Somebody's Anticipating Trouble

* The SAT was first known as the Scholastic Aptitude Test, then changed to the Scholastic Assessment Test. Today, the SAT acronym does not have a definition.

Dictating

"Did you sign up for the SAT?"

"The ACT?"

"Don't forget the subject tests!"

"When is that check due?"

"If you don't ask your teacher for a letter now, your application could be incomplete."

During the college application process, there's a pretty good chance you might become a deadline dictator. Your child should be taking responsibility and managing all of this, but sometimes it doesn't happen or you're too scared it won't.

What if you let the chips fall and she learns the hard way? There goes that guest room and your sanity. At times like these, maybe sticking your nose in a bit isn't such a bad idea.

Bribery

Before you veto the thought, remember the power of foil stars and Goldfish®? Sometimes parents have to bring in reinforcements to make things happen.

Because parental threats are often ineffective, finding the applicant's Achilles' heel can be critical in getting a little application momentum going.

The barter system (a toned-down version of a threat) can be quite effective. A draft essay for the car keys might be a fair trade. The opportunity to attend a basketball game might be worth a draft application. A draft is important because no one should hit the "send" button until the best product has been produced. This rarely happens during the first step of the bartering process, but a skeleton essay or application or résumé is a start.

Perfection comes with time and sometimes the task is more palatable in small steps.

● ● ● ● ● ●

SOME THINGS NEVER CHANGE

Somewhere in the college application process, I forgot that character traits are stable. Because it was important, I thought my senior would embrace deadlines and approach college applications with enthusiasm. When he said he would work hard and get his applications "out of the way," I thought that meant "completed"— not shoved under his bed. My nagging became a way of life. We had two totally different approaches to the same process. Mine: "Let's do this right and get it out of the way." His: "If it's in by the deadline, what does it matter?"

Looking back, I should have seen it coming. This was the same kid who asked where he could buy a corsage for his date 20 minutes before the dance. (Note: Corsages aren't just for proms anymore. There's another $35 that won't make it into the college fund.) He was the ten-year-old who announced at 9:30 p.m. on Wednesday that he needed a Styrofoam® ball and glitter by 8:30 a.m. on Thursday. He gets an "A" for consistency and an "F" for frustrating me. The good news? You can strategize, because teens are predictable. You don't need glue sticks or glitter at this stage of the game—just patience.

● ● ● ● ● ●

Other Parents

Let's take a break from complaining about kids and complain about other parents for awhile. If you think all parents of seniors hold hands and form support groups, now's the time for a little reality therapy. Not all parents are bad, but

<table>
<tr><td>Other parents
can be bullies.</td></tr>
</table>

it only takes a few to make you crazy. The college search does funny things to parents. Personalities become exaggerated and all bets are off. Some share helpful tips and insights. Others become competitive, secretive, and resentful. And fair-weather friends become your best friends, but only if you're an Ivy League alum. Other parents will help you, but it's hard to predict who they will be until you're smack in the middle of the process. There are five parent prototypes you're bound to bump into. Not all are pleasant, BUT you can learn from all of them. And don't panic if you see a little bit of yourself in each one. The college search can do that to the best of us.

1. The Truth Teller

What You Can Learn: Honesty and sharing can make a positive difference

This tell-it-like-it-is parent is honest and supportive. She doesn't sugarcoat the experience or her kid. She helps you realize that your senior's attitude isn't unique. If you're going through this at the same time, you'll swap stories and deadlines, voice frustrations, answer questions, and eventually celebrate together. If she's already been through it, her successes and failures will guide you.

2. The Doomsday Story Teller

What You Can Learn: Don't believe everything you hear

Misery loves company, but not when it comes to college admission. This story-telling parent is quick to share the woes of others, especially if they involve perfect standardized test scores, more volunteer work than Mother Teresa, and—can you believe it? —the inability to get into any top colleges. Exaggeration makes for more compelling but inaccurate stories, so don't panic; there are plenty of options for your child.

> **5 Ways to Avoid Being a Bad Parent Prototype**
>
> 1. Share the truth with other parents you trust
> 2. If you want to brag, keep it within the family
> 3. Limit your application involvement to proofreading
> 4. Don't go off the deep end with club and academic suggestions
> 5. If you tell a bad college story, counter it with a good one

3. The Imposter

What You Can Learn: Honesty is the best policy

The Imposter parent is a ghostwriter and, yes, a liar. He writes essays for his senior and even fills out the application. He's been known to use his senior's email to correspond with the admissions office. Sometimes he laughs about it and other times he justifies his actions because of that crazy busy senior year. Truth be told, the Imposter has been doing his kid's homework since middle school. Parents who consider helping their student in this way should know that ghostwriting can lead to college rejections.

> Truth be told, the Imposter has been doing his kid's homework since middle school.

4. The Résumé Jammer

What You Can Learn: More isn't always better

This pushy parent believes that the secret to perfect college applications is résumé padding. She's never met a club, volunteer experience, or an AP class that wasn't suitable for her child. If her kid had a needle phobia she'd still sign her up for the embroidery club. She usually learns the hard way how burning out your high school student can backfire.

5. The Aggressive Competitor

What You Can Learn: Stage mothers and fathers aren't your friends

I used to think that viciously competitive kids would grow out of it until I met their parents, also known as trainers. These are the pageant parents who've been shoving their kid to the front of the recital line since preschool. Some take you by surprise, like the close friend who isn't excited about your senior's success because hers hasn't gotten an acceptance yet.

It's normal to want your children to achieve college success, but Aggressive Competitors take inappropriate actions. They stalk teachers, coaches, and opportunities to ensure their child is always considered. They're not advocates; they're bullies. They warmed up on the bleachers of the kindergarten soccer games, screaming at their five–year-old to "buck up" and making snide comments about other children. The only difference now is that these parents have years of practice and are pushier and sneakier than ever. They'll ask for your child's test scores and GPA for comparison analyses so they can size up the competition or cry foul when your senior is chosen over theirs. The

Aggressive Competitor can also bring out the worst in you. Steer clear or you could find yourself bragging just to keep up or secretly hoping their senior hits a few roadblocks.

● ● ● ● ● ●

TOP TIP

Parents, "we" are not applying to college. You will naturally want to be involved as your child goes through the college admissions process—especially if you plan on footing the bill! However, you must LISTEN to what your child wants from the college experience, instead of projecting your own aspirations. (Sorry, your frat party is over! And if you didn't get into your dream school, that doesn't mean your child needs to apply.)

Dr. Katherine Cohen, College Admissions Expert,
CEO and Founder of IvyWise and ApplyWise.com

● ● ● ● ● ●

Chatter and Commercialism

For 17 years, you've reminded your kid how fabulous she is. She has the trophies and the ribbons to prove it. And now, everywhere you turn, someone or something is suggesting that, where college admission is concerned, she just might not be good enough. You can't turn on a morning show without seeing a feature on college competition, high rejection rates, and the astonishing accomplishments of high school seniors who are in the same applicant pool as your child. You're proud of her work at the food pantry, but how will she ever compete with the teen that fed a small country by raising millions of dollars via email? He even flew the food in by helicopter himself! (Apparently in between AP classes and fundraising, he had time for flight training.) Take a deep, cleansing Lamaze breath and stay calm. It's easy to second-guess yourself and your child when you're being hit from all angles.

● ● ● ● ● ●

TOP TIP

Choose SAT test prep very carefully. A lot of test prep is junk food—like trying to lose weight on a fast food diet.

Debbie Stier, Founder, PerfectScoreProject.com

● ● ● ● ● ●

Like it or not, your family is shopping. People are going to try to sell you something. And some of them will try to sell you one of the biggest ticket items of your life. It's your job to sit down with your child and figure out what's worth it and what's not. That goes for college and college prep.

Take an important goal (college acceptance), add some difficulty (standardized testing, essays, financial aid forms), a little mystery, and some media chatter, and you've got an opportunity for panic and money-making. Unfortunately, those who panic are usually the ones spending the money.

Believing there is only one perfect school can make you and your child more vulnerable to college commercialism and scams.

The college prep business is a multi-billion dollar industry. Some options are impressive, others useless, and still others are scams intended only to part well meaning parents from their cash. For every expensive option, there are effective, inexpensive alternatives. There are pricey classroom-based courses in standardized test prep as well as less expensive options, including online study, CDs, workbooks, and flashcards. Not all coaches and tutors are expensive. Experienced guidance counselors, teachers, parents, friends, and relatives with the ability to successfully support a senior through the college application experience can also help your child and your budget.

Be a smart shopper and do some detective work before you buy. Remember, money can't buy you love or college happiness.

By the time you've gotten through writing test prep checks, it's time for your teen to power shop. Students and parents often set out in search of the perfect college, when in reality there are many wonderful schools where a student will thrive.

Colleges and universities also want to be the chosen ones. That's why they send encouraging letters and brochures depicting happy students on a campus where the sun always shines and classes are primarily outdoors even if it is February in Alaska. (I made that up and have never seen an Alaska brochure, but you catch my drift.)

Believing that there is only one perfect school can make you and your child more vulnerable to college commercialism and scams and future disappointment.

A strong college application showcases accomplishments and potential.

Five Things Every College-Bound Parent Should Know

1. It's not always fun.

In fact, it's usually not fun. Big milestones, like applying to college, are rarely without some family conflict. It's normal, but it feels worse when it takes you by surprise. I asked my son's guidance counselor what he would tell parents about the college search. His simple reply: "It's not comfortable."

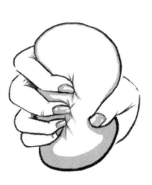

2. You may know a lot, but you don't know it all.

Granted, up until this point, it felt like you were a better decision-maker than your teen. But now there's a good chance your child is in an environment where college choices and the application process are hot topics. Some kids have everything under control. Some even know what they want. Don't assume you have all the answers. And even if you had the time of your life at Fill-in-the-Blank U, it doesn't mean she will.

3. More is not necessarily better.

More doesn't always mean better performance or opportunities. A student who is overloaded with academics and extracurriculars risks burnout. In the pursuit of being well rounded or covering every base, she may also lose the depth and niche that colleges find attractive. Likewise, more college applications may mean more opportunities, but more paperwork (and essays!) can zap an applicant's energy and drain submission quality.

4. Strategy and creativity can maximize application success.

A strong college application showcases accomplishments and potential. Sometimes a student needs to think outside the box when it comes to finding opportunities, pursuing interests or highlighting them. Encourage creativity and entrepreneurship from the beginning.

You probably know your college applicant better than anyone. That's why you may be the best predictor of how she will approach this process. Take that knowledge and strategize a little. Procrastinators are unlikely to be early birds, and overachievers probably won't turn lazy. Help your child move through the process in a way that will circumvent problems and won't turn you into the bad guy.

5. The messages you send are powerful.

It seems like they aren't listening, but the college applicant hears more than you think. Don't obsess about all things college. She's already nervous. Help her find and believe that there are many places she would love. Let your messages be motivating and sensitive, especially when you're throwing in a dose of reality. And don't get discouraged when you think she isn't paying attention. You just might be wrong.

• • • • • •

TOP TIP

Students are in charge and they will have options.

Jane C. Hoffman, M.B.A,
College Admissions Advisor

• • • • • •

Five Things to Tell Your High School Student

Share the following advice with your teen.

1. High School Counts.

Toto, we're not in middle school anymore! Grades have always mattered, but now they matter more. Part of the official transcript, grades are the most important piece of the package for college acceptance. A strong GPA should be a priority. While you will have an opportunity to explain lapses in academic performance, it's always best to keep your grades in check. You should tackle challenging courses and course loads while being realistic about your time and aptitude. Burnout doesn't help morale, anxiety, or the admissions process. And extra time and extra credit in the classroom counts. Take the points and get an edge.

2. Like your teachers (or at least some of them).

Life is more pleasant when you are around people you like. It's also easier to ask for and receive help, guidance, and recommendation letters from people who think highly of you.

3. Know your guidance counselor or guidance options.

A good guidance counselor can make the steps toward college application and admission easier. She's equal parts sounding board, motivator, reminder, and voice of reason. She doesn't have all the answers, but she has a lot of them. And if she doesn't know the answer, she knows where to get it. The better she knows you, the more equipped she will be to help you identify and reach your goals. Guidance counselors are often asked to write letters of recommendation for their students. If your school system is challenged and doesn't appear to have the financial capabilities or faculty to do college prep well, you will need to research other options. Speak with college students and their parents, family, and friends. Visit the National Association for College Admission Counseling's website (www.nacacnet.org) for student resources, planning tips, and consulting options.

4. Build your writing, public speaking, and technology skills.

Writing is an important and free outlet for expression and a valuable tool for success. A good writer can inspire and convince. When you are comfortable writing, you are less apt to procrastinate (that includes college admission essays!) and will feel more comfortable with some forms of testing. You may also find you have more time in test-taking situations. Writing well can help clarify and organize thoughts, develop vocabulary and give you an edge.

Public speaking can be anxiety-producing, but practice makes perfect. Speaking opportunities will help you gain confidence that can lead to better interview experiences.

Not many disciplines merge with everything, but computer technology can enhance just about anything related to education. Computer literacy can boost academic success by helping you strengthen project content and presentation. Even basic keyboarding can enhance speed and subsequent success. If you can quickly put thoughts "to paper" or, in this case, "to screen," you are at an advantage when it comes to productivity.

5. Be creative.

Additional opportunities for success can be found when you think outside the box. Whether it's identifying alternate experiences or finding unique ways to maintain good grades, creativity can open doors. Pairing creativity with volunteering, standardized test prep, or job searches can result in unique opportunities and solutions that can make you shine.

5 Things Parents Can't Live Without

1. Helpful parents who've "been there"
2. Guidance office phone number
3. Spell check
4. A break from thinking "college"
5. Patience

Parent Statement: "Let's talk about college!"

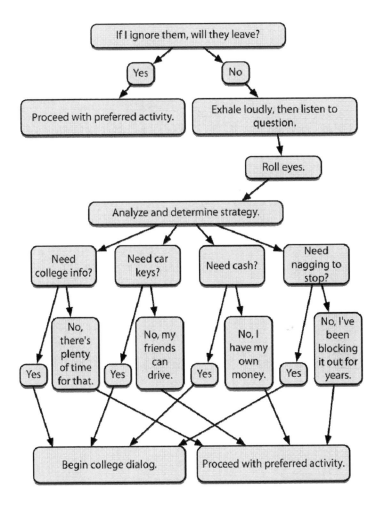

Figure 1: Teen Train of Thought

Now Relax!

Of course you feel like you're going crazy. You're sending your baby out into the world—or pretty close to it. And you want to know she'll be happy and successful. And, oh yeah, it's probably going to cost a fortune. Don't panic. As the parent of a college-bound child, in between being a cheerleader, proofreader, drill sergeant, travel agent, deadline monitor, loan officer, and voice of reason, you need to find the time and ways to relax. Take some tips from way back when. Schedule "time outs" with family. Arrange play dates with friends. Mandate naps. Take one baby step at a time and try to enjoy the ride.

2: STANDARDIZED ANXIETY

During my son's junior year, I woke up in the middle of the night sweating, but this time it wasn't from a hot flash. In my dream, or to be more accurate—nightmare—I was taking the SAT. I didn't have a pencil, a calculator, or a clue. (And I was naked and my teeth were falling out, but that's beside the point.) That's when I woke up and panicked. Was I a bad mother? I'd take a bullet for my kid but not the SAT.

Standardized testing can turn your life upside down. It can make the calm parent anxious, the grounded parent crazy, the frugal parent a spendthrift, and the quiet parent explode. In the college-bound process, standardized testing ranks at the top when it comes to parent and student stress. That shouldn't be surprising when you consider the facts. Like it or not, if a

Not all colleges require the SAT or ACT.

university requires standardized tests, a great score can sweeten the deal and a bad one can make you wish Junior's science fair project uncovered the cure for something horrible. Fear of the unknown is always worse than fear of the known. And except for maybe the Coca-Cola® recipe, is there anything more blanketed in secrecy than standardized tests? Add in those often shared "great students who've done poorly" stories, tack on a waiting period for results, and voilá—the ultimate recipe for insanity.

※ ※ ※ ※ ※ ※

TOP TIP

My best advice for getting your kids' vocabulary SAT ready? Read. And I'm not talking about your kids. I'm looking at you! Read challenging books, newspapers and magazines, then use any newly learned words around the dinner table. Hopefully your kids will pick up your reading habit, too. At the least, you'll be exposing them to tough words they're unlikely to hear elsewhere. When test day looms, their already beefy vocabularies will allow them to easily learn even more new words when they start serious prep for the SAT.

Jenn Cohen
President & Chief Word-Nerd
www.Word-Nerd.com

※ ※ ※ ※ ※ ※

Other factors fuel the fire of anxiety. Some students take the test once. Some take it five times. Some prep like crazy. And some just act crazy about prepping. Your mailbox and inbox are flooded with suggestions that your child will do better if you buy something or hire someone. Even if you value the products and can afford them, you are then hit with the reality check; buying the prep product doesn't

> No scientific study has confirmed that expensive prep methods get better results than inexpensive ones.

mean your kid will buy into it. If I used the SAT to describe my children's pretest attitudes toward my attempts to "help," it would have to be S (stubborn), A (apathetic), and T (testy). Giving ACT equal time, their personalized acronyms would have been A (anxious), C (cranky), and T (threatened). It's hard to know what to do and where to begin to be a helpful parent while maintaining your sanity and 401(k). Take a deep breath and let's walk through the steps together.

5 Panic Busters

1. Talk to a great guidance counselor
2. Mark test dates in your family calendars
3. Read College Unranked*
4. Consider colleges without test requirements
5. Take a nap

* *College Unranked: Ending the College Admissions Frenzy.* Edited by Lloyd Thacker. Harvard University Press, 2004.

There are 4 P's to the standardized testing process: Panic, Preparation, Performance, and Put-it-Aside. Full-blown panic is painful, but a little can be good for all involved. It can shift

> Some students score better on the ACT. Some students score better on the SAT. Some students score the same.

people into gear and on to strategic planning. Prepping isn't fun but if chosen wisely and utilized—which is the operative word when a teen is involved—it can result in decreased anxiety and an increased sense of control. Performance is all about test taking and with some preparation, this can be maximized. Put-it-Aside is what students and parents must do once the test is taken. Obsessing about standardized testing after the test is not helpful. Regaining a little normalcy is in order, even if it only lasts a few days.

P Is for Panic

Panic isn't pretty, but it's pretty normal. Between fear of the unknown, deadlines, time lines, and timed tests, parents and teens can feel pummeled and confused. Corral your teen, gather information, and proceed with optimism. It's a learning process for all the players.

Clueless

It's hard to identify a college's standardized test requirements if you don't know the college. For every student who has a neatly constructed list of favorites drawn up before junior year, there are a hundred others who have no clue where they want to land. Their parents are the anxious, clueless type wandering around the college fairs looking for support groups.

> Don't sign up just because everyone else is doing it.

Realize that choices may be slow in coming but that once their peers start moving forward, most students will follow. Either way, for most applicants and parents, standardized testing is a necessary part of your life. Many colleges require applicants to take either the ACT or SAT[1]. Additional tests like the SAT Subject Tests™ may also be required.

5 Methods of Encouraging Practice

1. Discussing its importance
2. Choice (student picks study format)
3. Bartering (1 hour of study for 1 hour of video games)
4. Bribing (no practice, no party)
5. Captivity (car rides with vocabulary word lists)

So, is the SAT or ACT mandatory for admission? No. Some colleges and universities do not require standardized testing and others are moving toward eliminating it. But if your child hasn't mentioned these schools, or if he wants many options, he will take at least one of these tests and should be prepared for the experience. Identify the testing dates and put them in student and parent calendars.

---

[1] At this writing, all schools accept the ACT and the SAT.

• • • • • •

STANDARDIZED ROAD TRIPS

The last weekend before Dan's senior year, our family drove from Pittsburgh to Michigan for a wedding. This was a desperately creative parent's dream come true—six hours of uninterrupted family time and a few good hours of captive attention. We had SAT scores to boost! Armed with my new vocabulary-driven RAP, Rock, and Blues CD and accompanying lyric sheet, we hit the highway. For the sake of score elevation, I cranked the stereo to a full 24. Forget the eardrums; my senior would remember that, in the world of standardized testing, the phoenix is a bird and not a city. After about three minutes, Dan's little brother tried to help him climb out the sunroof. The lesson: road rage doesn't necessarily involve two cars.

• • • • • •

Test Prep Options and Other Parents

It happens slowly. The postcards begin to arrive at the end of sophomore year. All proclaim they can make a difference. And the difference always involves 100 points MORE...never fewer..."guaranteed." Postcards morph into packets as junior year approaches and application anxiety rises. The parental buzz begins. Bleacher chatter about expensive review options, coaches, tutors and prestigious universities is enough to make you run out for a blood pressure check and a bank check. Take a deep breath, do some yoga, or wear earplugs. There are thousands of ways to tackle most problems and that goes for standardized test prep. What works for one student may not work for another. There are many options that address different types of testing needs and different budgets. Prices range from free to exorbitant. The good news: No scientific study has confirmed that those who spend excessive amounts of money on college prep fare better than those who use less expensive methods or none at all. It all depends on the student.

Getting Testy

Sometimes the only thing worse than worrying about your teen's test taking is the thought of taking the test yourself. If the last test you took was a blood test, then chances are you'll be more frightened than your child when you look at a practice SAT or ACT.

Remain calm. Parent anxiety is common and normal, but keep it under wraps. Sure, that's hard to do when there are so many cues to make you question your child and your parenting. Thumbing through test prep materials freaked me out. Those page-a-day math calendars stirred up post-traumatic stress from the '70s. The vocabulary drills left me speechless. And I had the answer key!

That's when I realized, as a parent and psychologist, it was time to stop putting myself in the equation. Here's the good news—most high school students do more algebra, geometry, and essay writing than their parents. They've been living in a test zone and this is more of the same. Sure, the content and the stakes may be different, but it's still about tricky problem-solving, concentration, and number 2 pencils. Relax and allow them to do their job.

• • • • • •

It's a Bird. It's a Plane. It's SAT Mom!

Every now and then, you meet someone who breaks the stereotype. Enter Debbie Stier, former publishing house power-house who has made it a personal mission to get the perfect SAT score. HERSELF. Chronicling her incredible journey on PerfectScoreProject.com, she's got her number 2 pencils sharpened and a team of test gurus on speed dial. Debbie's that rare parent allowed to roll her eyes and say, "Tell me about it" when her teens whine about test prep. As tempting as that might be, I'd rather stick pencils in my eyes than have to use them to fill out those answer bubbles. Thankfully, I have a direct line to Super SAT Mom.

• • • • • •

The Apathetic Applicant

Even though I'm sure test anxiety has a genetic component, it's easy to feel like your kid is taking the SAT or ACT and you're the only one panicking. College is such an exciting opportunity, yet when I tried to talk with my college-bound kids, they often looked about as enthusiastic as a patient coming out of anesthesia. Trying to pull college prep enthusiasm out of a high school junior or senior is like talking to a sleepwalker—which might be close to the truth, given the teen sleep-wake cycle. And just when you muster up sympathy (it's hard to make room for practicing in the middle of a busy curriculum and social life), he wastes 15 minutes making fun of the math tutor. Repeat the following during times of frustration: "Parent-child conflict is normal and painful. Soon he will be in college and I will miss him."

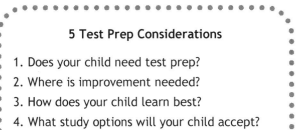

5 Test Prep Considerations

1. Does your child need test prep?
2. Where is improvement needed?
3. How does your child learn best?
4. What study options will your child accept?
5. What options can you afford?

What About the Dream School?

Test scores can influence admission. And sometimes scores fall within a range that make a student less competitive. Sometimes it's another factor. Regardless, parent and applicant can benefit from a new mantra: "There is more than ONE perfect place." Dream schools can be nightmares if the match isn't a good one or if school priorities differ from the applicant's. And when dream schools are your dream and not your child's, a nightmare could be brewing. Back-up plans don't have to be second-rate and, for many, second and third choices turn out to be the best choices.

P Is for Preparation and Performance

If I survived test prep, so can you. I've threatened, negotiated, and bribed, all for the sake of superior scores. Sometimes it worked. Sometimes it blew up in my face. Through snooping, shopping, and nagging, I learned how parents can make big differences and why sometimes, they make the situation worse.

The true secret lies in being realistic about your child, your budget, and your involvement in the process. If you run the risk of ruining your relationship on the road of college prepping, back away and bring in reinforcements! And lower your expectations just a little; expecting enthusiasm and pleasantries from a student in prep mode is just plain crazy.

I've toyed with the idea of paying for college tuition by inventing toys college-bound parents would appreciate. The SAT Barbie® would come with a tutor and a dream house in lockdown until she raised her score 100 points. That pink Jeep® wouldn't leave the driveway unless it was headed to a Kaplan^{SM} class. ACT Ken® would come with a bad attitude and flashcards. He'd be sold separately and wouldn't be allowed to visit Barbie until vocabulary drills were completed for the day.

But I'm pretty sure my Standardized Testing Parent Action Figures would be the best sellers. The four types, based on the common approaches parents take in test prep would be sure to strike a chord with problem-solving parents everywhere. I was three of them.

The most costly standardized test prep program is the one that isn't needed or used.

The Purchasing Agent Parent (PAP)

...comes with a tote bag and a line of credit

An overachieving problem-solving optimist could go broke in the test-prep phase. The PAP launches into the process full force. There are so many options—programs, classes, tutors, coaches, online learning, books, CDs, DVDs, and flashcards. Some are bargains. Some are costly. Some are helpful. Some are useless.

The PAP is a wishful thinker. She believes that all prep-related materials have the potential to inspire or boost her child's performance. She can't pass a Barnes & Noble^{SM}

without buying the latest set of flashcards to reduce her own anxiety. Her motto—"If I buy them, he might use them." Wishful thinking can fill a house with hope, exercise gadgets, and test prep materials. Stacks of phonebook-sized prep books force the Ab Roller® to the attic.

If you're a PAP, slow down and do a little research before you purchase. You'll spare the college fund and have room for a treadmill.

The Drill Sergeant Parent (DSP)

...comes with a stop watch and throat lozenges

This action figure is focused and tough as nails. The DSP takes action in many forms. From enforcing sign-up to drilling and quizzing, she makes sure preparation is happening. She's on alert for test prep diversions and is quick to shut down Skype™, instant messaging, and Guitar Hero® if they're infringing on study time. She lurks outside bedroom doors and can bellow out warnings from two floors away.

She'll withhold the car keys from a teen if commitments aren't met.

When the Drill Sergeant is in charge, there's the tendency to make the whole family sweat. The DSP has been known to put the entire family in lockdown for prep (nothing like revving up that sibling resentment) by banning electronics, media, and well—anything fun until test day. This can send a harmful message to the test taker—this is the most important thing in the world and you aren't capable of mastering it without severe environmental changes. And the message it sends to other children in the family can be equally damaging—"Your brother's test scores are more important than your needs right now." Panic may whip you into action, but don't let it turn your home into standardized testing boot camp.

The Desperately Creative Parent (DCP)

...comes with index cards and glitter

The DCP has always opted for do-it-yourself options to showcase her unique talents and cost-effective style. She struggles with the facts and calculates her student's strengths and weaknesses to find study options that won't cause a meltdown. She handwrites word lists and tries to make the unpleasant fun. She'll tolerate ridicule and eye rolling as she pitches the possibility of an SAT Scrabble® game she invented herself. Her creativity focuses on slipping in prep materials when they are least expected and detected.

Creativity worked well for our family but not without student sarcasm. Recognizing that vocabulary building is key to improving the critical reading score, I became the linguistic Martha Stewart. Instead of frosting cupcakes a thousand ways, my meals were served with thousands of vocabulary words. I tossed them into conversation, drizzled them onto random sentences and used them to spice up bland stories. To be honest, most words I had never seen. If I used them often and correctly, my only friends would be Kaplan tutors. If I'd put this much

attention into my own achievement, I'd have a Nobel Peace Prize and a house in the Hamptons. My son's critical reading score did improve, but I'm not sure if it was my technique or the fear of having to retake the test and endure more mealtime vocabulary treats that inspired him.

The Obnoxious Other Parent (OOP)

...comes with bullhorn and scrapbook

The OOP will drive you crazy. In between bragging about heavy AP loads and Ivy League connections, she is busy providing you with all the details of her child's prep program, including schedule and cost.

The OOP's child is even more talented than yours, because he is able to squeeze prep classes in with all the other overachieving accomplishments in his life. OOPs can make you second-guess your parental decision-making and dedication to your child's college-bound journey.

If you are worried that you might be an OOP, you're probably not. That's because OOPs don't have time to worry; they're too busy talking about their kid's college admission potential.

So Many Options, So Little Time

Test preparation can be beneficial for most students, but student prep needs can differ. Prep can include process (understanding the test experience), content (teaching to the test; e.g., tutoring), and strategy (understanding test construction and scoring). Some students will benefit from covering all bases. Some need only strategy. And a chosen few will sail through the process with nothing but a powerful knowledge base and incredible self-esteem. Reading more about the standardized test process and the specific tests and talking with guidance counselors will enable you to help your student make better choices about preparation and testing.

There is no "one size fits all" test prep weapon. Every student is different. You can break the bank and your back on these opportunities for your child, but that doesn't mean he will embrace it or pay attention. He can find the best tutor in the world "ridiculous" or decide he won't listen to the course instructor because he wears "weird shoes". In times like these, logical counter explanations and thoughtful parental suggestions are rarely welcome.

Pick your battles and test prep selections carefully. Encourage your student to identify options and evaluate them according to his test needs, learning style, schedule, and family finances. Success won't happen if he doesn't take part in the process.

ACT.org and Collegeboard.org offer economical online ACT and SAT prep.

> **5 Reasons to Consider a Program or Tutor**
>
> 1. Your student has test anxiety
> 2. Your student needs preparation
> 3. A structured format may enhance learning and discipline
> 4. Parent-child collaboration would be a disaster
> 5. There's a good chance spending money will guilt him into prepping

Sometimes "to prep or not to prep" is a real question. Junior year is chock full of academic intensity and most universities agree that grades are even more important than standardized test scores. For this reason, anything that takes away from school studies should be carefully considered. Examine the pros and cons of prep options with your child before choosing.

Countdown Time

You know tomorrow is test day when your child hesitates just a little before asking for the car keys, mentioning the birthday party he MUST attend, or asking to have a few (more than five) kids over. Don't stir up the anxiety, but don't

Sacrificing grades for standardized test prep weakens the college application.

facilitate an all-night adventure at the expense of test performance. One more day to go. One more night to be a good parent, which doesn't necessarily mean being a popular one.

● ● ● ● ● ●

STANDARDIZED INFOMERCIALS

One day, there will be test prep infomercials. A fancy online program with Nobel prize-winning alums will go up against another team who pairs the student with hot tutors resembling the latest TMZ sensations. Both guarantee 100-point increases in scores. If you order within the first 30 minutes you get a free Chia® Pet for the dorm room. Smart parents will analyze both programs, want the Nobel option, but order the opposite. That's because showing up is the first step to good prep. Trying to impress the tutor doesn't hurt either.

● ● ● ● ● ●

Test Day

I know it's early, and it's probably easier to hand him the car keys, but you may want to consider driving your child to the test. Sleep-deprived student drivers with a little test anxiety are prone to traffic accidents.

Parking problems and limitations can also make a student late for testing. Dropping off your teen will give you peace of mind that he arrived and—unless he hid out in the bathroom—took the test.

Wish him luck, try to be upbeat, and then go out for coffee.

● ● ● ● ● ●

'TWAS THE NIGHT BEFORE SATS

'Twas the night before SATs, when all through the home,

No one was chillin', except the lawn gnome.

The pencils were sharpened; the ticket was bought.

But my student wanted an 11 pm curfew, and that's when we fought!

"This isn't negotiable," I said with a sigh.

"You can't tell me what to do," was his only reply.

So I hid all the car keys and camped out by the door,

Tossed him a prep book, and paced the tile floor.

When out on the lawn there arose such a clatter,

I sprang to action to see what was the matter.

Away to the window I flew like a flash,

Tore open the shutters and threw up the sash!

There in the cul-de-sac all in plain sight,

Were three other families in SAT fights:

"No Facebook®." "No Twitter™." "No Skype and no Wii™."

"Go flashcards." "Go practice tests." "Go rest—No TV!"

From the top of their lungs, to the top of our own—

It all was so crazy, I dropped my cell phone.

And then in a twinkling, it all got quite clear—

They'd all be in college this same time next year.

Parents got tearful, but secretly cheered.

The teens stopped pushing and halted their jeers.

They spoke not a word, as they left their front yards,

Sharpened more pencils and studied flashcards.

And now that it's over with college in sight,

We all sleep much better and wish you a good night.

Watch the video on DrNancyBerk.com

● ● ● ● ● ●

P Is for "Put It Aside"

When the test is over, it's time to hang up the advisor hat you've been wearing and give it a rest. Everyone's exhausted and deserving of some peace, even if another test date is in the future. Celebrate your student's accomplishment. It isn't easy being in the test chair.

Settling the Score

Is once really enough? If two times is good, is four times better? Some applicants take the SAT or ACT once. Others take it more than four times. All hope to improve their scores, and a few shoot for a perfect score. Counselors suggest that unless the score is fabulous, the student should take the SAT or ACT two or three times. Not retaking it after one weak score, may be viewed as a red flag, suggesting a lack of motivation. Taking it more than four times might present a different red flag. My son's friend announced he was retaking the SAT because he "missed one." He would have had a perfect score had it not been for one pesky question. He signed up to take it all over again. I wanted to ask if it was really worth it. But then I realized I could sleep in because he'd drive my son to the test. I bit my tongue and wished the brilliant overachiever good luck.

You've Got Mail

Remember the relief of having a test behind you and the escalating anxiety a week later when the teacher started passing out the scored tests? It's no different here, except the wait is a lot longer and the stakes seem higher. Refrain from constantly quizzing your teen about the score release date; it will only enhance the tension. If you need to keep an eye on the process, put the date in your calendar. And let your teen own the scores. It will be hard, but they're not yours to open or broadcast. Whether the scores are perfect or less than optimal, don't throw them around for public consumption. These are personal pieces of information that belong to your child. Disclosure is his decision. If you must brag, brag about his work ethic, not his scores. If you must complain, complain about his tendency to sleep until noon, not his test scores.

⬤ ⬤ ⬤ ⬤ ⬤ ⬤

HOLDING IT UP TO THE LIGHT

My husband and I got the house and vehicles all to ourselves when Hunter left for a ten-day spring break trip with the Spanish Club. We looked forward to whine-free living and a rest from our interrogation duties. Only one thing stood between us and carefree living—Hunter would be away the day his SAT scores hit the mailbox. Suddenly there was a chore he forbade us to do for him. Under no circumstances *were we to open that envelope.*

Respecting teen privacy is important and difficult. And it's next to impossible when it involves an acronym that has been in every dinner table conversation for the past eight months. I begged before he left. I would open it, but not say a word. I would open it, but not tell him I opened it. I would be positive and upbeat, no matter what the scores. All scenarios were rejected. I was not to open his mail. It was illegal.

"Is it a felony to open someone's mail if it's your kid's SAT scores?" I asked my husband, probably the only person on earth who felt my curiosity pangs.

He muttered something about "loco parentis," but he's a doctor not a lawyer. I shelved my plans to break any laws, because I wasn't sure if he was talking about a medical condition or some legal loophole he inaccurately picked up on *Law & Order*.

My "vacation" was restless as I summoned the willpower to walk away from something harder to ignore than Halloween candy. I considered the power of steam and the invention of halogen bulbs, but forced myself not to go there. At day three, life was bearable but only because temptation had yet to be delivered. I closed my eyes and prayed. Please let snail mail live up to its name. And if it doesn't, please let the envelope be very, very thin....

* * * * * *

Give Back!

Once testing is over, give your child and yourself a pat on the back and focus on giving back. Be a positive parent. Let other parents know the tension and anxiety will pass. Don't be secretive; share your strategies and tips for success. Inform the guidance counselor about specific courses and products that were outstanding or disappointing. If your house looks like a Princeton Review^{SM} Satellite Office, it's time to take action.

In 2009, my 16-year-old son Hunter began the College Bound Collection (CollegeBoundCollection.com) a college prep book drive initiative that now includes schools from all over the country. He quickly found that 95 percent of donated study guides were in mint condition. Were these tools gently used or never used? Perhaps they reflected the search for the "right" prep tool. Sometimes a student needs to review a few resources before he finds what works for him. Whatever the reasons, parents were thrilled to donate and more than a few shared similarly revealing information—"Maybe someone will get some use out of this. My kid didn't even open it." Guidance libraries in these schools can now provide all students with access to test prep materials.

Find homes for prep materials that are no longer needed. Books that are outdated or well used can be sent to the recycle bin. Materials that have barely been touched can be donated to high school guidance offices, libraries, and programs that will put them in the hands of needy students. Imagine the room you will have! Then go celebrate with your teen, because this milestone of anxiety is over.

3: YOU'RE GROUNDED

For years you've used the term "you're grounded" as a parental threat, but now you're the one who needs to get grounded. It's easy to get caught up in the whirlwind of college, the excitement of a new adventure, and the desire to help make your child's dreams come true. It can be difficult to keep your feet on the ground, but staying mentally, physically, educationally, and financially logical is critical to creating a supportive environment for the college-bound teen. Some parents can do it on their own. Others need a little help. Whichever way, find what works best for your family.

Give Me Guidance

It's not always pleasant being in foreign territory, but there's plenty of help for teens and parents if you know where

> Not every parent and child can sit calmly at the table and chit-chat about college essays.

to look. Get ready to ask questions, no matter how foolish they seem. And there's nothing wrong with asking for help. Not every parent and child can sit calmly at the kitchen table and chit-chat about college essays. Knowing your family dynamics and your abilities and limitations can help you find the best solution for your teen. Good guidance is important for student success, whether it comes from you or another knowledgeable and caring source.

The Guidance Office

A student should meet and begin to know her guidance counselor freshman year. This is the time to learn of career and college resources within the school and to confirm that a student's academic track is consistent with her college goals. While the student should be meeting with the counselor on her own, having a parent-child-counselor meeting at the end of junior year or beginning of senior year can help all involved get on the same page before the application process kicks into full gear.

> Good guidance is important for student success.

Some parents have the guidance counselor on speed dial, but not all high schools have counselors or impressive guidance. In these situations, families have more work to do. Finding mentors and advisors can be a challenge, but they exist in the community, the classroom, and online. Speak with successful graduates and their parents, enlist the help of teachers you and your child respect, review other schools' websites for college-bound guidelines, and start strategizing.

● ● ● ● ● ●

TOP TIP

A good consultant says to parents and kids, "Let go of the hype."

Deena Maerowitz, J.D., M.S.W,
Founder, Undergradadmit.com

● ● ● ● ● ●

Study Guides

Will using a consultant, coach, tutor, or program give your child an edge in the college process? Maybe. But you'll never really know, because there's no controlled double-blind study to prove it. Either you use one or you don't.

Whether your student is looking for support from a college consultant, coach, tutor, commercial counseling center, or website, it's all about credentials. Options come in all different shapes, sizes, and price ranges. Their motivations can differ. Like any service industry, there are probably more good than bad. Most want to help, but some are more interested in your check.

Research the options like you would a babysitter. Examine qualifications. Ask questions. Make sure your teen likes them. In speaking with dozens of college consultants, I was struck by their insight and dedication to supporting students. Some waive their fees for needy students. Others specialize in helping children with disabilities meet their goals. And some will help parents find other professionals better suited to meet their child's needs. There are wonderful consultants, tutors, coaches, and programs, but identify them before you pull out the credit card.

● ● ● ● ● ●

TOP TIP

College students are an untapped resource in regard to tutoring. If you are on a tight budget, a college student should only cost you between $15–25 an hour. Here are two pieces of advice. When hiring a college tutor, check to see if they have experience working in the college learning center. Secondly, ask for a recommendation from a professor. A recommendation from a professor should usually give you some insight on their maturity and punctuality.

Eric Clark, Founder/CEO,
Quincy Tutor Network,
www.quincytutoring.com

● ● ● ● ● ●

Will using a consultant or program make your life easier? It definitely can if the guidance is good and your child embraces it. It won't if you spend half the time arguing with her about attending appointments and following advice. And it definitely won't if the guidance is bad.

What if you don't hire anyone to help your child? Plenty of people don't. I didn't, but I also had the advice of consultants at my fingertips, thanks to their books, websites, and social media. It's all out there if you take the time to dig, read, and learn.

● ● ● ● ● ●

TOP TIP

Successfully getting into college and being successful in college simply require preparation—not one year of prep starting in 12th grade, but 12 years of prep starting in first grade.

Akil Bello, Co-Founder,
Bell Curves (bellcurves.com),
the Educational Services Company

● ● ● ● ● ●

Five Ways to Get Free Expert College Advice

Please refrain from being a pushy helicopter parent when using these options.

1. Twitter

Follow colleges, admissions professionals, coaches, and prep experts. Follow chats (e.g., #CampusChat) and get answers to your questions without writing a check.

2. LinkedIn®

Join groups on LinkedIn that relate to college prep, admissions and parenting college kids. Interact with professionals, parents, and students. You'll meet great characters without a character limit.

3. Facebook

It's more than a party place. Check out specific college pages. Many college experts also have Facebook fan pages where they share tips and strategies.

4. Email

College experts often provide contact information on their websites. If you have a specific question or need a reference or resource, send them an email.

5. Fee Waivers

Many experts will adjust their fees if a true financial hardship exists. Ask, but be honest. If you're driving to the session in a Porsche®, don't go there.

Money Alert

Parents and kids are exhausted by the college application process and once they're done, it's tough to get teens to fill out another application even if it involves receiving money. Examine scholarships early in the process. Ask your child to obtain scholarship information from the guidance office, including local scholarships. Review the tips and guidelines for scholarships offered on www.fafsa.ed.gov, the government website for the Free Application for Federal Student Aid (FAFSA). Do not fall prey to scholarship scams. When you see red flags (like being charged to apply for a scholarship), run in the other direction.

Child Development

No, this isn't about developmental stages; it's about helping your child develop and organize a plan to showcase herself in an optimal and honest way. There are so many pieces to the puzzle. And it can require extra organization and effort if your child's college application requires a specialized portfolio (e.g., film and television, musical theatre, photography, sports). Parents who can help their teen stay organized will find the process less stressful. There are just two problems. Not all teens want the help. And not all parents know how to be helpful.

* * * * * *

TOP TIP

Be your child's biggest cheerleader and encourage him/her to do his/her personal best throughout. Get to know your child's guidance counselor. Help create a college checklist with deadlines. Accompany your child on college visits, while taking a back seat and allowing him/her to ask questions.

Dr. Katherine Cohen, College Admissions Expert,
CEO and Founder of IvyWise and ApplyWise.com

* * * * * *

Niche Marketing

Colleges now seem to be looking for students with a niche. In our day, the well rounded student was in demand. We scrambled to check all the boxes and told our kids to do the same. And now they tell us universities prize a well rounded student body comprised of driven, passionate students with specialized talents or niches.

Don't panic. Every college wants to look good. Your child must show them what she will bring to the plate. Help her think outside the box when it comes to her talents and interests. Encourage her to explore additional opportunities where she can demonstrate growth and highlight her skills. Look at her activity list and résumé for themes. You might just see a niche.

Clubs

Clubs and extracurricular activities were invented for exploring and pursuing interests, not for résumé padding. Some students overextend themselves, because they genuinely crave involvement. Their activity lists are large and legitimate. Other students show up for one meeting and the "right" to call themselves a member. Whether fueled by a pushy parent or a slick student, résumé jammers annoy active club members who bear all the weight. If you're tempted or think your teen is contemplating that route, think again.

There's no need to super-size the résumé.

Honesty is the best policy when it comes to the résumé. And the admissions professional is like a cross between your mother and a polygraph expert. Her mission is to get at the truth;

and she's usually pretty good at it. She's seen stacks of résumés, lists of impressive accomplishments, and lists of lies. Résumé jammers get caught when their recommendation letters, interviews, and essays highlight the contradictions. It's hard to chat comfortably about a club you only went to once.

There's no reason to be at a loss for résumé material and there's no reason to have to super-size anything. Some activities are more demanding than others. Some students have obligations that prevent them from participating. Relax. Colleges get this.

Does your teen whine about school club options? Call them "stupid"? Suggest that the Spanish Club is a front for watching hours of soap operas (which is another effective way to learn the language)? Have you heard every reason on earth why there is nothing for her? This is the perfect time to encourage her to take it to the next level. While this might mean looking outside of school for opportunities, it can also lend itself to creating a school-based activity. Some administrations welcome student-founded clubs. Encourage your student to channel her interests in a way that illustrates initiative, leadership, productivity and creativity.

Jobs

My younger son has been an entrepreneur since the age of four when he persuaded his college student babysitter (who was as attractive as Jennifer Lopez) to help him assemble a lemonade stand. They made $35 and sold out in an hour. He thought he was salesman of the year. Looking back, maybe he was marketing man of the year, thanks to the patronage of every teen boy on the cul-de-sac who coughed up 25 cents for a little Crystal Light® stirred by Jenny from the block.

Since then, he's been quick to accept jobs and create ones when the opportunities present. At age 12, he left for summer camp with $40 and returned with $75. Apparently the snacks and beverages I supplied for his consumption became the inventory for a camp convenience store located in the bottom bunk. Part of me was horrified and another part proud that he had found an opportunity for employment.

Kids learn a lot about themselves when they work. College applicants should never dismiss their job experiences as unimportant. (Okay, maybe leave out the camp concession sales.). Every opportunity brings a teen closer to finding out where she wants to be.

● ● ● ● ● ●

My Teen, My Personal Trainer

It seemed logical. My teen wanted to earn money and I needed an external push to keep me on track with my exercise routine. Why not reinforce his ambition? His price was better than my last trainer's and his eagle eye and persistent nature were befitting a fitness guru. Other than pounds and body fat, what was there to lose? I kept a diary....

DAY ONE: Today was a lesson in teamwork. My trainer was my biggest cheerleader, coaxing me down the exercise trail and gently reminding me of my nutritional obligations. Could it be that when it comes to food and fitness, adolescents are stronger and have more conviction than their parents? They certainly receive dramatically different lessons in health class. I still wrestle with the voice that reminds me to clean my plate while my son can do a monologue on the terrors of trans fat. He popped in a "motivational DVD" as I did my time on the treadmill today. Hoping for an upbeat music video, I was instead treated to the vivid documentary *Super Size Me*. Smart kid; I was fascinated and disgusted by drive-thru food facts. Suddenly I'm driving around town in search of a smoothie. No more empty calories for this girl!

DAY TWO: Never hire a personal trainer who laughs at you while you are doing an exercise DVD in the den.

DAY THREE: How could the child I once carried (and got a whopping varicose vein in the process) refuse to throw me a stray french fry? Things are getting a bit tense around here. I find myself hiding out from my own kid. It isn't fun having a personal trainer who eats almost every meal with you. I flirt with the idea of closet eating but opt to send my trainer to his room for annoying me.

DAY FOUR: Apparently there are four forbidden food groups when your teen is your trainer: 1) high fat, 2) high calorie, 3) processed, and 4) theirs. Eating from the fourth food group is a double violation.

    PT (Personal Trainer): How could you eat the LAST piece of pizza? That was going to be my breakfast!

Me: Sorry Mr. Personal Hypocrite Trainer. I just couldn't help myself.

DAY FIVE: How I have lasted five days in the presence of a dictator that I empowered is beyond me. Fortunately, his interest is fading faster than my waistline.

PT: Mom, I'm thinking you might want to get a real trainer. I'm just not into it.

Me (thinking silently to myself): Happy Days! But I must be sensitive. I don't want him to feel badly about this early work experience.

Me (out loud): I'm sorry; I know I'm not the BEST client. I appreciate all your help, but I think I can do it on my own now.

Fortunately, seemingly logical but bad ideas blow up in your face quickly. This keeps us from driving down the wrong road for too long. What you learn along the way can be frustrating, funny, and valuable. While it's important to involve your adolescent in healthy activities, any time you blur the lines between the roles of parent and child, problems emerge. No child needs his mother or father as a client. I'm sure I'll re-examine that position if my son becomes an enormously successful investment banker. Meanwhile, this mom will be boarding the treadmill solo, where she plans to watch a harmless hour of *The View*.

❋ ❋ ❋ ❋ ❋ ❋

Regardless of the position, working is a powerful résumé builder and can be as influential as any formal summer program. But more importantly, having a job is character building. Loved or despised, a job is an opportunity to learn responsibility, develop interpersonal skills, and explore personal values and interests. Recognizing that she never wants to do a specific job again can prevent your teen from going down the wrong path in the future.

Some students are unable to pursue extracurricular hobbies because of the need to work. Admissions officers recognize this and consider these job experiences to be as valid as sports and clubs in the student profile. What if the job is less than glamorous? Don't worry; a history of fast food service can be more impressive than a summer working for mom's prestigious law firm, because it implies the applicant isn't coasting on connections and last-minute résumé padding. Admissions officers will see beyond job titles, but the application and résumé must give them a true picture of the student. Encourage your senior to think beyond and behind the job as they tell their stories.

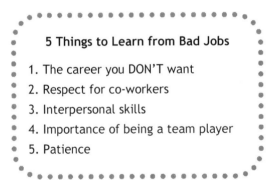

5 Things to Learn from Bad Jobs

1. The career you DON'T want
2. Respect for co-workers
3. Interpersonal skills
4. Importance of being a team player
5. Patience

Volunteering

Most high school students who complain about volunteering don't lack empathy or compassion. Sometimes they're just teenagers encountering one more thing that makes them feel put upon. It doesn't help that their plates are full with academic and social obligations, and of course ALL those chores that you "make" them to do. The importance of volunteering can get lost when parent-child tug-of-war begins. Thank goodness many high schools require volunteer hours to graduate. Now teens can have rewarding mandatory experiences that they can't blame on their parents.

Giving back is important. Communities and lives depend upon it. Life lessons learned through volunteering are endless and surprising. Eyes and hearts are opened to others, but volunteers also see themselves more clearly. Strengths, weaknesses, and talents come into view. Sometimes even simple discoveries help with the bigger picture. A hospital volunteer quickly realizes he can't stand the sight of blood. That may be unpleasant and throw a ringer on those pre-med aspirations, but it's valuable information to have. Volunteering with young children might inspire some to pursue teaching careers and others to run for the hills. Even reluctant volunteers can find something positive or heartwarming in the experience.

> Life lessons learned through volunteering are endless and surprising.

* * * * * *

THE JUNIOR AND THE COBRA

"How was it?" I asked my junior, who had just returned from a mandatory tutoring gig with first graders.

He had shuffled off with the "whatever" attitude, not expecting to learn anything. After all, he was doing the tutoring and the situation seemed to border on boring. Then he met his feisty charge.

He told the story better each time, marveling at the stubborn conviction of a seven-year-old who didn't want to do homework any more than my teen wanted to take an SAT practice test.

"I asked the kid his name and he jutted his neck out like a cobra and just hissed at me."

"Mmm hissing can be problematic. Did he do his homework or just stay in reptile mode?"

"Well, he wasn't very cooperative, but I finally figured out a way to get him to do his math problems."

I panicked for a second. What if he had used me, the frustrated college-obsessed parent as his role model? The school wouldn't take kindly to a tutor making threats, even if they were idle. And of course they wouldn't approve of paying the child. I hoped his repertoire was better than the "write the essay or else" tactics I used on his brother.

"And your solution was...?"

My son was beaming. "After dozens of attempts, I made him think he was missing out on some fun competition. I just pulled out my cell and told him it was a shame, because I was timing him. He suddenly began doing his times tables."

And so, two hours of tutoring forced a junior to problem-solve to help a child. And he enjoyed it. You've got to love the power of volunteerism. And you've got to marvel at the power of the iPhone®.

✳ ✳ ✳ ✳ ✳ ✳

The most fulfilling volunteer experiences for students and recipients are those infused with enthusiasm and hard work. Going through the motions and clocking the hours isn't true volunteerism; it's work release. Volunteering early in the high school career is always beneficial. It may also lighten senior year requirements and prevent scrambling procrastinators. Students should also keep track of volunteer hours for graduation requirements and college applications.

Teens can give back by doing what they love. Whether it's facilitating a club-based volunteer project or developing an opportunity for others that involves sharing their unique talents, the best volunteer opportunities are generated by sincerity and enthusiasm. Help your teen find unique and exciting options.

5 Unique Volunteer Projects

1. Magic lessons at a children's hospital
2. A community service podcast
3. A quilting marathon to benefit homeless shelters
4. Computer instruction for the elderly
5. A music video for a non-profit

The Cyber Image

You may not be computer savvy, but as a parent you must be savvy about your child's computer footprint. Impression management extends beyond the classroom and the interview. Anything about her that hits cyberspace really can go "to infinity and beyond."

Decades ago, when parents coached kids on how to make a good impression, they issued hygiene reminders, dress code rules, and a few conversation starters. Today there's an additional detail that's trickier and scarier to address—your child's "cyberlife."

Your teen's image isn't just about what she creates; it's also about what her friends, acquaintances and enemies create and post about her. Helping manage this can be difficult for a teen and impossible for a parent who may have no knowledge or access to this information. It used to be you could dress to impress, but if the internet has captured your child in various stages of undress, someone's going to be doing damage control.

What teens find amusing today can be googled by college officials and employers tomorrow. In cyberspace, a sensitive, conservative, pre-college brainiac can be transformed into an out-of-control party girl. No one cares that the red plastic cup had orange soda in it or that the bong was just a joke. If someone misinterprets your teen's joke, the joke's on her.

Even little things can damage an image. If your teen's email address begins with "hotbabe" or "luvmyvodka," take immediate action and insist on a new address.

The Transcript

College-bound high school students should always follow the most challenging academic path that showcases their aptitude and accomplishments. Some parents and students think the most competitive transcript is the one stacked with every available AP class. This isn't always the case. Excellent grades in AP classes can boost a GPA, thanks to weighted scoring, but sometimes the grades aren't good.

> Volunteering early in the high school career is always beneficial.

AP loading can be parent- or student-driven and can backfire if not carefully analyzed. Really bright juniors who take on AP calculus aren't always cheery when the semester also includes AP Physics, and AP US History, especially if the subjects don't interest them. AP may mean "Advanced Placement," but to some it can feel more like "Another Pressure." Burning out mid-semester is dangerous for a teen and a transcript.

The Résumé

Not all colleges require a résumé, but putting one together lets a student see her paper image. It can also be a helpful document to provide to recommendation letter writers and her first shot at self-marketing.

The applicant's written snapshot, a résumé should be honest and flawless. Sometimes a comprehensive activity list can work just as well. Either way, these documents should capture the energy and enthusiasm of the applicant. A strong résumé is driven by solid academics and interesting extracurricular experiences.

Professional résumé writers, expensive printing and exaggeration can't replace on-the-job education, after-school activities, and excellent course choices. And being hokey is risky. Tie-dyed paper is eye catching, but few reviewers will be amused by a Woodstock-inspired résumé. While this is the time for polish, high gloss could also send the wrong message. And super slick can just be slippery where college applications are concerned. Does a $12 color copy photo

> Burning out mid-semester is dangerous for a teen and a transcript.

résumé say "I care," "I'm rich," or "My dad's PR firm made this for me"? Think before you spend or send.

The first draft of a résumé or activity list always fails to tell the full story. That's because teen and parent memories can't pull it all together in one sitting. Even the most detail-oriented will realize an important missing piece a few days later. If you're allowed, take a look at your student's draft.

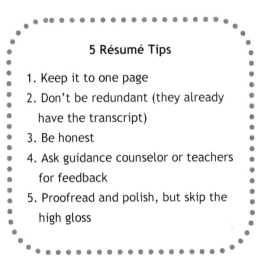

5 Résumé Tips

1. Keep it to one page
2. Don't be redundant (they already have the transcript)
3. Be honest
4. Ask guidance counselor or teachers for feedback
5. Proofread and polish, but skip the high gloss

You might recognize that she neglected to mention her work with the basketball team or the nursing home project freshman year. Two heads really are better than one, and when you highlight something positive, sometimes a teen is appreciative.

* * * * * *

TOP TIP

Preparation prevents panic. Those who are prepared for the college process when their child enters high school will be less stressed and anxious when application time comes around.

Suzanne Shaffer, College Prep Expert, Founder,
ParentsCountdowntoCollegeCoach.com

* * * * * *

Clutter Management

Remember before you had kids, when your dining room table was empty and you didn't have to waste hours rummaging through stacks of papers in search of an overdue permission slip? Me neither. And it gets worse during the college application process. Staying semi-organized will save chunks of time later. Below are some easy tips to keep everyone on track.

Signing on for the college search releases the floodgates of all things paper, so it helps to plan ahead. It's challenging making order out of paper chaos, but it can be pretty simple. An old cardboard box, a handwritten checklist, and a designated corner can get you there, but some parents and seniors gravitate toward slick office supply options.

The college search releases the floodgates of all things paper.

Retailers are more than willing to help you color code your way to college. Snazzy file folder holders. Paisley print boxes with matching clip boards. Specialized notebooks and calendars. Any system will do, so long as someone uses it. If your child isn't organized, this is the time to teach her this important skill.

The Accomplishment Box

If you're the type of person who always put her photos in albums the second you got them, skip this section. This advice is for people like me, the ones who took tons of photos of their kids but still have them in a shoe box somewhere.

The Accomplishment Box is your holding chamber for documentation of high school accomplishments. An empty photocopy paper box will do. This box will spare your family hours of frustrating searches and memory-wrenching recall. It is not for university brochures or test prep materials; it is the landing pad for anything that your teen might want to include on a college application.

What goes in the box? Anything that documents talent and commitment—even an index card with a note, "edited the football team game videos."

Other contents should include school transcripts, brochures and descriptions from special programs or classes, drama, band or chorus concert

programs, volunteer verification forms, honors and awards, press clippings, outstanding high school writing samples, CDs of performances, artwork, videos, and portfolio pieces.

The contents will help jar your child's memory and yours when résumés are being written and activity forms are requested from guidance counselors or recommending teachers. It will be a "go to" place as college applications are being completed. Paper tossing can happen later, but for now, this box should hold anything that could potentially help the applicant create a complete picture of her high school experience and college potential.

The Paper Chase

Information overload is in full swing with a college applicant in the house. You have more catalogs and brochures on your dining room table than Pottery Barn® has in its mailroom. The dining room table is so far gone, you've booked a reservation for Thanksgiving dinner. It's an anything-but-green feng shui paper nightmare.

Encourage your child to make a detailed "to do" list.

To solve this, your motto must be "Look, Toss, or File." Unfortunately, seniors like to toss without looking, or look and then toss somewhere into the abyss that is their bedroom. Pre- or post-dinnertime sorting can be the perfect time to get a grip on paper confusion together.

Coordinated Calendars

Sure your teen should keep track of deadlines, but what if she's so laid back, it could hold her back? Standardized test dates, application deadlines, and graduation-related events and requirements are set in stone. I know what some experts say, but as a parent, I say "put it in YOUR calendar too." Teens are busy and scattered and two memories are usually better than one.

With my own memory challenges (thank you, estrogen, for leaving me at a time when I needed you most), I needed a large paper calendar to track graduation and college-related deadlines. Given the length of the search and application process, a monthly calendar, like the ones included in charity mailings, work well and give you a big visual overview of what lies ahead.

5 Dates to Record and Flag

1. Honor Society application deadline
2. Standardized test registration deadlines
3. Standardized test dates
4. Letters of recommendation due dates
5. Transcript request deadlines

See the college prep calendar by the National Association for College Admission Counseling (NACAC) for monthly breakdowns of steps and suggestions in the college application process. (www.nacacnet.org) This free and informative timeline can help parents and teens create structure in these deadline-driven times.

The Power of Lists

I've always been a list maker. If I were as compulsive about completing my "to do" lists as I was about creating them, I'd be Oprah by now. But regardless of the speed of your actions, lists can be powerful tools to help you visualize the tasks at hand and plan accordingly. The college application process is a daunting, multi-stepped task that intimidates many. Encourage your child to make a detailed "to do" list. It can clarify each step and illustrate time demands without parental nagging.

● ● ● ● ● ●

SCIENCE FAIR CENTERPIECES

I've never understood why the cotton gin always gets tagged "best invention" and the dining room table is never nominated. The best multi-tasker in the world is the dining room table. It's been decades since it was used for its intended purpose in our home and it's still indispensable. Thanksgiving 1996, my youngest son proclaimed, "Wow, maybe we could eat here again sometime." I should have given him an honest reply like, "Sure honey, right after you graduate from high school," but he was four and I didn't think he could handle it.

I was also naive and optimistic, never recognizing that our life would require a six-foot-long table to hold papers, projects, and gift wrapping expeditions. The only time sugar cubes have made it to our table was for a third grade Alaska project. The only chargers ever to rest there were phone-related.

Over the course of the last 17 years, my dining room table has held more paperwork than the DMV and more poster boards than Staples®. During senior year, the table became the centerpiece for the college war room. It was a logical choice, because applications must be pristine and, ironically, the dining room was the only place in the house where food stains would never occur. That'll change mid-June when we clear it off for the graduation party. Maybe we'll find enough sugar cubes for the iced tea.

* * * * * *

The Application File

As application time nears, there is often activity on multiple applications. This can lead to confusion, including essay swapping. The application file is critical for preventing frustration and panic. This file should contain multiple labeled folders, including one for each university application and essays (even partial essays in the event of an electronic malfunction). Another folder should include copies of the résumé and activity lists for review, as well as for distribution to teachers for recommendation letters. A folder for the high school transcript and course-related documents is also important, along with an additional folder for copies of all completed essays. Keeping these materials in one place will decrease the possibility of important documents going M.I.A.

So, now just when your feet are planted securely on the ground, it's time to travel....

4: SEARCH AND SEIZURE

In the ideal world, your teen comes up with a list of eight potential colleges. You veto one for price, one for party reputation, and one for distance. (Because even if you could afford it, an airline ticket with three connections isn't prudent.) You're left with five; you visit three or four, and you're done. Sounds pretty simple unless your child is the strong, silent type. Trying to get an early list of colleges out of my younger son was like chatting with a mime. Twenty questions later, we were no closer to pinning him down on any campus possibilities. Talking to other parents in the same boat of indecision, it became clear this is a common phenomenon. Not only is the reluctant college list maker relatively silent, when he does speak, his selection criteria borders on ridiculous. Here's a verbatim transcript from my life....

Me: What about Texas?

Teen: I don't think I can go anywhere where they speak with Southern accents.

Me: But you have a Pittsburgh accent; this really isn't the place to start throwing stones.

Me (after deep breath): How about Ohio? There are so many great schools in Ohio.

Teen: I'm not going anywhere that borders our state.

Me (rough calculations look like he's eliminated five additional states and Ontario; I am determined to figure this out): And why is that?

Teen: It just doesn't feel right.

Conversation closed and no closer to creating a list.

5 Conversation Starters

1. What is the ideal college size?
2. Do you prefer a large city or a rural setting?
3. How far from home would you like to be?
4. Do you have a major in mind?
5. Which college friends love their schools?

Your student is supposed to drive the process, but if he won't kick into gear, it's hard to find a starting point. Before you throw in the towel and assume you'll never get that extra guest room, read on and discover how to nudge your applicant forward.

Get a Big Book

Those enormous college guide books allow you to quickly compare similar statistics and facts across schools. While statistics won't give you the full picture, these phonebook-sized resources are a great starting point. College coaches suggest strategically placing them around your home to increase the likelihood your teen will browse.

● ● ● ● ● ●

TOP TIP

Do thorough college research whether visiting, on the Internet or speaking with students and admission representatives. Prioritize the factors most important to you in a college and make sure the college has what you want. Finding your right college matches is crucial! Once you have your working college list, stay organized, know all requirements and stay on top of dates and deadlines. Think of quality over quantity in writing essays, listing activities, gathering recommendations and when compiling your college list.

Jeannie Borin, M.Ed.
Founder & President
www.college-connections.com

● ● ● ● ● ●

Cruise College Brochures

Brochures and other materials can highlight the unique and outstanding features of a college. They give you insight into points of academic excellence, student body composition, and the community. College brochures can also be examples of marketing at its finest—testimony to the impression that everyone is happy, attractive, intellectually challenged and enjoying the sunshine. Like the sugary cereal ads that captivated our preschoolers, university marketing tools can sway students and parents. If a perfect picture meant a perfect fit, this would be easy. Unfortunately, real college life isn't airbrushed. Make sure information gathering comes from more than one source.

Virtual Reality

No shoes. No collared shirt. No problem. Virtual college tours are free and easy and without dress codes. Whoever said, "You had to be there," really didn't consider the value of virtual tours in getting some of the legwork done. If you're dealing with budgets, time constraints, or the need for more information, these free options are worth the trip. They can help identify and answer questions, determine tour itineraries and provide a springboard for valuable real life tours.

• • • • • •

TOP TIP

Students need to shop like colleges do. When they are shopping, they are empowered. That's a good thing.

Jeannie Borin, M.Ed.,
Founder & President,
www.college-connections.com

• • • • • •

Visit school websites and take their virtual tours, then move on to others. YOUniversityTV.com has over 3,000 college and career videos. CollegeProwler.com and Unigo.com are two outstanding student-driven college search sites. My favorite Unigo feature—students can match their interests and characteristics to schools. My favorite College Prowler feature—their "by students for students" emphasis reminds teens they are consumers and have a voice.

The beauty of browsing and taking online tours? They're free and you can visit in your bathrobe. Warning: Many of these sites cover information parents might not want to think about, but probably should (e.g., dating, drinking, and drugs).

Fair and Balanced

When it comes to connecting, college fairs give you the most bang for your buck. Encourage (or push) your teen to explore, chat, and collect business cards and ideas. He should also take advantage of university visits at his high school. These visits are wonderful ways for applicants to balance their schedules and still stay on the college radar. Remind your student that these professionals are often involved in the selection process. Even if students have scheduled a campus visit, it pays for them to show up at the guidance office, meet the rep, and be memorable in a good way.

● ● ● ● ● ●

FUN AND GAMES AT THE COLLEGE FAIR

When the college fair came to town, I was ecstatic. Clarification was in our future. For a few hours and a small parking fee, my son would have the chance to visit hundreds of schools and pick the brochures and the brains of admissions reps everywhere. He was game, but only if his father and I maintained a 100-yard distance from him and his college-bound girlfriend. Once again, we were victims of the Parent Restraining Order. Realizing this wasn't about us, we agreed and unleashed the happy couple into the collegiate convention center. After a few childless moments, I prayed we had made the right decision.

The fair didn't have a midway, but there were plenty of sideshows to keep us entertained. Annoyed, eye rolling students trailed pushy, well meaning parents. A mother-daughter team walked arm in arm from booth to booth in their matching Ugg® boots and hair extensions. Groups of unsupervised teens patrolled the hall, more interested in a hot pretzel at the concession stand than a university revelation. Some booths buzzed with applicant interest while others appeared sadly unpopular. Parents nudged reluctant kids into lines and others decided it was easier to just get in line themselves. One parent described his daughter's approach as "take the pamphlet and run."

Childless parents, we visited college booths anyway, hoping our son was doing the same and not just walking the perimeter to keep us quiet. But our ability to keep our distance could only last so long. What if he didn't talk to the great rep at booth #220? Would it hurt for him to just swing by #75 and ask a question?

My husband and I looked at each other and nodded. The Parent Restraining Order does not apply to text messages. I grabbed my phone and typed furiously.

Text #1: You will be walking home if you don't visit Blank University.

Text #2: If you don't have the brochure, I won't believe you stopped there.

Text #3: And grab a soft pretzel if you're hungry; we're not stopping for food on the way home.

● ● ● ● ● ●

Get the Financial Picture

The college search has to be approached with some financial realism. Look at a financial range of schools that will enable you and your child to make informed decisions when the time comes. If, after examining financial aid and scholarship probability, a college is out of the realm of possibility, be upfront about it from the beginning. There's nothing pleasant about telling a senior, after he's been accepted to his top choice, that he can't go.

Being realistic early in the game will prevent heartache later. Some parents forget that you can take out loans for college, but no one will give you a loan for retirement.

Stay in touch with the big picture, because there is more than one future to fund. That being said, make sure you investigate financial opportunities before you exclude a school.

• • • • • •

TOP TIP

Before eliminating expensive schools, parents should calculate the cost for their family. The good news is this can be easily done thanks to net price cost calculators that every school must post on their website. These calculators provide an estimate of actual cost after parents submit financial data, teen's test scores, and GPA. By using this, teens can focus on schools within their budgets. These calculators will empower families by making college costs transparent and that's long overdue.

Lynn O'Shaughnessy, best-selling author,
speaker and consultant, who writes for
US News & World Report, CBS MoneyWatch
and The College Solution

• • • • • •

Map It Out

Looking at a map can be eye opening. Sitting down with it and drawing an acceptable college radius can be a conversation starter.

Some parents and students have clear geographic guidelines based on finances (e.g., flying is cost prohibitive, so colleges must be within a five-hour driving distance) or other personal factors like medical conditions.

* * * * * *

FINDING COLLEGE BUDGET-BUSTERS

In a *USA Today* front page feature, journalist Oliver St. John uncovered unique budget cuts crossing campuses for the 2011–2012 academic year. Among them: eliminating phone lines for professors, asking professors to take out their trash, and making students pay for printing. As a former full-time professor, I'm okay with emptying my trash and limiting phone time. And as the parent of college kids, I'm fine with paying for paper and ink. Here are a few more creative suggestions to help universities save a few bucks....

1. Cancel a course or two.

I know college is supposed to be fun, but will "The History of Blue Bubblegum" or "The Rise and Fall of Charlie Sheen" really give my kid an edge?

2. Cut the printing costs for admission materials.

Use the four-point font from the tuition and financial aid section throughout the entire brochure. This should save at least four pages.

3. Decrease your photography budget.

Eliminate those pricey outdoor shots of the happy cross-section of students sitting in the grass on a sunny day with an engaging professor. It's a nice touch, but after awhile, every college admission brochure looks the same.

4. Stop building.

Consider following your outdoor photo concept and hold more classes outside. Students and professors seem really happy.

* * * * * *

Multiple Choice

College selection is like a multiple choice test with more than one right answer. When it comes right down to it, great opportunities are everywhere. There are nearly 2500 accredited four-year colleges and universities. And still, parents and students continue to panic over finding and getting into the "right" college. Not everyone gets their first choice, but nearly 80 percent of college freshmen rate themselves as satisfied or very satisfied with their college experience. So, regardless of college acceptance and rejection, the majority of college applicants land in places where they are content.

Having more than one great option is critical, because applicants can't predict what a college is looking for in any given year. Seniors need to be reminded that rejection is not a reflection of their inadequacies. There are plenty of people who are happy and successful with second choices. Many will tell you their second choices were often their best choices.

• • • • • •

TOP TIP

Work with your teen to compile a list of schools to visit. Prioritize them. Then start with the school that is his/her least favorite and work your way up the list visiting the first choice last. You'll be surprised at what you all learn along the way.

Z. Kelly Queijo, Founder, President
SmartCollegeVisit.com

• • • • • •

Going Local

Do students choose far away colleges because the grass is always greener on the other side or because parents aren't there? Living within physical nagging range is something many teens avoid like a cheap cell phone. Of course, it takes but a few moments of separation to learn that parental nagging doesn't require face-to-face contact.

We sometimes take for granted the beauty in our own back yards, and college selection is no exception. Staying close to home doesn't have to mean forgoing a true college experience or giving up a rewarding campus life. People sometimes don't discover the best parts of their town until they have visitors or become local college students. One of the perks: Living at home while attending a college can save a student as much as $10,000 per year.

Regardless of whether local options are part of your child's college plans, exploring nearby schools is an inexpensive way to gain insight into teen preferences like campus size and academic options. Along the way, you're bound to discover some local gems, interesting opportunities, and opinions that may help in creating that college list.

5 Local Pros

1. Access to family resources
2. Easy parent access to student events
3. Familiar location
4. Existing support network
5. Save money living at home

Reasons to Look Local

1. When the School Is a Good Fit

Local school options should be researched like long-distance options. If the school fits the applicant's criteria for academic offerings, campus size and type, student body, and extracurricular opportunities, there's a good chance the experience will be positive.

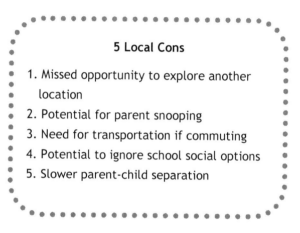

5 Local Cons

1. Missed opportunity to explore another location
2. Potential for parent snooping
3. Need for transportation if commuting
4. Potential to ignore school social options
5. Slower parent-child separation

2. When Looking for Good Financial Options

Not all local options are less expensive, and certainly financial aid and scholarship packages may result in financially attractive options far from home. But if finances are a significant concern in obtaining a college education, local institutions should be explored.

Be sure to investigate whether local tuition incentives are offered for residents.

3. When Parent-Child Boundaries Are Respected

Sometimes it's easier said than done, but going local also means that parents and students aren't thrown into a situation that demands immediate physical separation. This may be great, but it also can be the prescription for relationship disaster as college freshmen begin to demonstrate independence and make mistakes their parents likely made. Sometimes ignorance IS bliss. Long-distance parents may be able to keep anxiety at bay, because they don't know when their kids sleep through a class or pull "all nighters" cramming for an exam. Local is a fine option when both parent and student can set and respect boundaries and communicate well.

* * * * * *

Do Almas Matter?

Parents of first-time college-bound teens hug their kids a little tighter and wistfully plan tours that scream "bonding opportunity." I hugged my kid a little tighter because that's the only way I could keep him in the room long enough to plan a college tour. After an eternity of teen indecision, my husband and I created a plan. The first college road trip would be a double header—we'd take our son to visit our alma maters. He'd be able to compare a big university to a smaller one and we'd walk down memory lane together. Killing two birds with one stone sounded like a good idea.

Towering cornfields framed the country road, as we approached the beautiful campus of my alma mater, Denison University. I held my breath waiting for a sarcastic *Green Acres* comment from a teen I assumed preferred big city living, but he shocked us.

"Now this is cool. I love cornfields."

My husband nearly choked until the second sentence came out.

"Of course if there's no 3G, I'm not getting out of the car."

Fortunately, the quaint little town must have realized who ruled because there were five bars. And I'm not talking about alcohol.

As we toured campus on our own, I was admonished for pointing out landmarks. "Please stop," he pleaded. "Your pointing is condescending."

Pointing at a building is condescending? Apparently my point is an "over point," which is much more obnoxious to teens than an "under point."

My husband chuckled until we got to his Ohio State stomping grounds. That's when our son announced it had not made his list because it looked, well, "too much like Ohio."

In the end, though, in spite of teen "logic," our family walked away with a great comparison trip that generated talking points and a smidge of teen insight. He identified some significant preferences (beyond the "under point") and verbalized them. The moral of the story: You can kill two birds with one stone, but not without some squawking.

❋ ❋ ❋ ❋ ❋ ❋

College Connections

Encourage your teen to network with friends who are attending colleges of interest. These "experts" have lived where he might be next year. Getting details about teaching formats, resources, and accessibility can help guide applicant decisions. Do advisors really advise? Are there adequate activities outside the university? What about student mentoring? There's nothing like peer informants to get a student thinking.

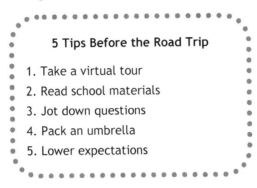

5 Tips Before the Road Trip

1. Take a virtual tour
2. Read school materials
3. Jot down questions
4. Pack an umbrella
5. Lower expectations

Hard Labor

The college tour process can be a little like childbirth. First you must endure an uncomfortable drive. And once that's over, the pain gets worse. Arguing is common and if insults are hurled, they're usually aimed at the ones you love most. After childbirth, you get a beautiful baby. After a college tour, you get to drive back with your teenager, who sometimes will act like a baby. The best part is, like childbirth, the pain fades fast. When all is said and done, those crazy tour memories will make you laugh and smile. But buckle up; it could be a bumpy ride.

I was all jazzed up for college tours. For some reason I had transferred my fond college memories onto the family college road trip. Images of cobblestone and parent-child bonding fueled my enthusiasm. We would sip lattés in the student union and people watch. The ride home would be a lively, productive dialog outlining campus pros and cons. Like a crazy woman, I had shelved the past 17 years of kid car rides and vacation reality. I practically burned a CD disco mix and rented a convertible.

College tours are exciting in theory, but like vacations, children don't always share our enthusiasm. If kids can throw tantrums and wish they were elsewhere in the Magic Kingdom®, then why do parents expect harmony on the college road trip? It's normal to want sunshine and rainbows, but unrealistic if family travels have always leaned a little toward *National Lampoon's Vacation*. There's one universal secret to college road trip sanity—lower your expectations.

Don't Become Shirley Partridge

Panic or obsessive-compulsive tendencies can put families on the road of perpetual touring. I call this the "Partridge Family Effect." Fear of missing something—the perfect college, a dangerous campus, a bad fit of any kind— can make parents and applicants believe that 20 tours are better than four. But touring is only a glimpse, not a guarantee.

Slow down. Stay calm. Plan carefully and don't overdo. You'll be less likely to burn out the family or burn up the credit card.

There may be power in numbers, but for college tours, sometimes less is best. Splitting experiences between parents can allow you to divide and conquer and maybe even live a little of your own life. If, like good mom Shirley Partridge, you're into multi-tasking, you'll want to ignore that suggestion and take the whole family on your bus.

Of course, there's nothing like adding a whiny younger sibling to the mix to keep you on your toes. Yes, this could save you from having to tour the same place again in a few years. But beware—trying to keep everyone happy can be a real parental chore.

* * * * * *

TOP TIP

Students who can't afford to visit a college of interest should be honest with the school. Use outreach opportunities like off campus interviews and receptions and inquire about programs that might allow you to visit the school.

Perry Robinson, Vice President
and Director of Admissions,
Denison University

* * * * * *

Let Them Drive the Bus

The college-bound kid can be a pain, but parents aren't entirely blameless either, especially when it comes to the college search. We can be overbearing, over-invested and over-the-top ridiculous. Most of the time, we don't even realize it. Take, for example, the subtle shift from "you" to the "WE" word as in....

"WE're applying to schools with strong engineering programs."

"Ideally, WE'd like to end up at Stanford."

"WE're touring the top six schools in New England, because we really want to end up on the East Coast."

The problem is, WE aren't going to college. (And I am so sorry about that, because it would be kind of fun!) We are facilitating the process and maybe subsidizing it, but this isn't our show. Provide input on itinerary and push a little when you believe they should consider a great option or omit a highly unrealistic one. Discuss questions before a tour, but let your child ask the questions. Don't dominate a tour to the point that others think you're the applicant or your teen is incapable of thinking for himself. Be a great parent guide and let your applicant drive the college tour bus.

Clothes Check, Rain Check, Reality Check

"You can't be serious," my son cried, as his father surfaced for the tour with a Bluetooth® on his ear and a bulging fanny pack around his waist. Stuffed with sunscreen, ChapStick®, and loose change he'd been collecting since the '70s, this accessory could convince clinging kids everywhere

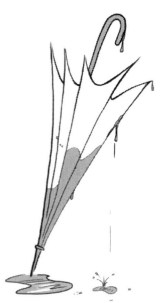 to head to the opposite coast for an education. To avoid these types of catastrophes, college tour preparation must involve wardrobe review. You don't need to be a personal stylist to realize the frayed band logo t-shirt isn't a good choice for the applicant. And you don't have to be Heidi Klum to know that the applicant's father should move beyond the "I don't get out much, so I'm strapping everything I might need to my body" look.

Some touring parents won't make good fashion choices, but that doesn't mean you should blindly follow. Expect parental fanny packs, black socks with white sneakers, and overdone desperate housewife moms in halter-tops and eight-inch gold heels in a rainstorm. For the sake of your child and a little bit of dignity, try to fly somewhere in between.

5 Parent Fashion Don'ts

1. Your daughter's jeans
2. Fanny pack
3. Dress shoes with khaki shorts
4. Tube tops
5. Tube socks

Speaking of rainstorms, there's nothing like a little drizzle to take the enthusiasm out of the applicant. You can drive 300 miles or fly across the country to visit their dream school, but throw in a little precipitation and that dream may die. There's a reason glossy college brochures include only sunshine and smiles. Pack an umbrella and skip the Sea World® poncho.

Caution: Parents on Campus

All parents embarrass their kids—some just do it a little better than others. Maximize bonding with your kids by vowing not to become one of these parent prototypes on your campus visit....

1. The Hipster

This isn't the young adult urban middle class Greenwich Village dweller-type hipster. This is the guy with the unbuttoned shirt and gold medallion. He'd still be wearing bell bottoms but no store carries them and he refuses to shop vintage. Often sporting Italian loafers (no socks), a tan, and superior attitude, he rarely talks unless name dropping or giving orders.

2. The Tourist

The tourist favors Hawaiian shirts but can pull off the look by just showing up. He would never carry a purse, but always travels with a bulging fanny pack. (Hello! The fanny pack is a waist purse!) The tourist delights in photographing all family activity and isn't embarrassed when inconveniencing others in the process. He'd hold up traffic for days to get the perfect shot.

3. The Turn-Around Teenager

From behind, they look exactly like 18-year-old girls, but when these moms turn around, teen boys everywhere just feel foolish. From their "yes, they are my daughter's jeans" with peeping thong to midriff-baring halters and Lady Godiva extensions, these moms specialize in crossing the line. They continue to channel their youth by flirting with their kid's guy friends. The Turn-Around Teenager Dad probably exists, but he's a lot less colorful and may go unnoticed.

4. The Verbalizer

Verbalizers are equally distributed across gender. They ask questions that make kids and other parents cringe. They've been doing it since preschool, so they're armed and dangerous. They fire off questions like their lives depend on it. Somewhere along the line, someone told them they'd get extra points for ridiculous. The Verbalizer also delights in waiting until the question and answer periods have just about wrapped up, then throws in another stupid question that no one can answer.

5. The Hoarder

Hoarders take anything that's free. Bottled water. Sandwiches. Brochures. It doesn't matter if they are thirsty, hungry, or in need of information; they don't want to miss anything. Married male hoarders are more prone to volume hoarding, because they have wives with purses to carry their stuff. The most dangerous? Married male hoarders with fanny packs.

The Tour de Chance

Yes, there's a chance you could land on campus and your teen will refuse to get out of the car. It's pretty common, totally baffling, and goes something like this....

Son: I've seen enough; let's go.

Parent: But we haven't even parked the car yet.

Son: You don't think I can tell already? I DON'T like it here.

Parent: But we're finally here. Let's get out and look around.

Son: Nope. You go ahead if you want to. I'm just gonna wait here.

So what's the solution? The easiest one is to respect the illogical teen refusal. After all, some claim if he is miserable at first sight, he will be miserable for four years if you force the issue. Do I agree? No, but have you ever tried to pull a 6 foot tall 17-year-old out of a parked car and make him follow you around campus? This is when gentle threats, reasonable bribes, and guilt ("Do something for me for a change!") come in handy.

Mortified

Remember when they were toddlers and idolized us? Probably 99 out of 100 teens are embarrassed by their parents. Even rock stars embarrass their kids without trying. It's unlikely your family will be spared, because it takes so little to make this happen. Take talking, for example. You can embarrass a teen by talking too fast, too slow, or too much, but never too little.

There are worse things than being ignored!

My son's tour embarrassment was certain, given my chatty nature and the fact that his otherwise quiet father is a "Line Talker." Line Talkers are the people who stand in line and try to break the ice with complete strangers. ("Where ya from?") Line talkers are sweet and well meaning, but a total teen embarrassment.

During college tours, parental line talking and just plain talking can result in TSA (Teen Separation Anxiety). TSA occurs when parental talking and other behaviors (wardrobe challenges, bad hairstyles) make the teen so anxious, he separates from you. Don't panic if your teen literally keeps his distance. Mick Jagger's kids probably gave him the same treatment. Face it; sometimes even great parents can't get no satisfaction, but they try and they try and they try and they try....

Time Out!

You probably have a lot of questions, but tour parents should be silent observers as much as possible. Questions should be limited to important topics that won't embarrass your child. This is not the time to ask about the availability of condoms at the health center or the phone number for the mental health center's crisis hot line. (Important sensitive questions can be asked privately.) If you are fortunate enough to be able to sit in on a real classroom experience, remember parents are not being graded on participation!

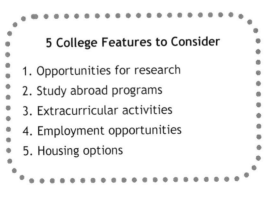

5 College Features to Consider

1. Opportunities for research
2. Study abroad programs
3. Extracurricular activities
4. Employment opportunities
5. Housing options

This is an exciting milestone and you've invested at least 16 years of your life to get here. Yes, Grandma would love to see this, but for the sake of family harmony, keep the camera in your pocket unless it's your teen's idea. If your child would rather take the SAT again than hold up the tour while you have him pose in front of the student union with his mother, then take a mental picture.

Tour Guides

Tour guides are selected to be a positive reflection of their university. Intelligent and helpful, they, along with a well organized tour, can provide applicants and parents with a great snapshot of the school. Their perky dispositions, great hair, and genuine school spirit can sell some of the most skeptical teens on the planet. When you bond with your tour guide, magic happens. Applicants consider the possibilities, and parents think about how lucky their kids are to have these opportunities.

Every now and then, a tour experience is disappointing. It's not unusual for guides to be hit with overbooked tours, obnoxious parents, straying students, and uncomfortable questions. On rare occasions, the only problem is the guide. Whether he's clueless, aloof, or so comfortable with the group that he's sharing inappropriate information, the situation can be disappointing. When this happens, try to maintain enthusiasm and explore the school after the tour. Visit the student union and the libraries. Walk around campus and observe on your own. Share a laugh and maybe even a latté with your teen as you review the day.

Teen "Logic"

The verdict is in and it's far from logical. The campus can be breathtaking and the tour guide engaging, but don't assume your teen's impression will reflect that. Rejection rationale is not logical or consistent across high school juniors and seniors. Rejection reasons are often bipolar. They include:

"Too many beautiful students—it's not normal."

"Too many badly dressed students—it's not normal."

"Gloomy weather—totally depressing."

"Too much sunshine –totally distracting."

During tour experiences, parents wait for logical academic rejection reasons, like "The library is outdated." Instead they are bombarded with reasons related to fashion, temperature, food, and architecture ("too much brick"). For some, a great tour experience involves pizza by the slice and a perky tour guide named Chloe. One friend was perplexed by the value her daughter placed on dormitory bathroom configurations.

> Expect "The Look."

Still, seemingly ridiculous rejection reasons are easier to understand than the vague one most parents hear—"I just don't like the look." Teens can't explain it, but they are 100 percent certain from "The Look" that this college experience will be the worst one. Expect "The Look," accept it, and drive on. You just might smile instead of scream.

* * * * * *

ROYAL DISAPPOINTMENT

When the Princeton Review releases their top college rankings, they also include a ranking of schools with "Dorms Like Palaces." Hold the tiara and armor. Before your teen squeezes on the glass slipper or buys a white horse, it's best to beware of college castle-dwelling surprises. Royal dorms aren't what they're cracked up to be. Sure, on the surface, there's that stuffy elegance that screams "cul-cha," but one must always consider the drawbacks. Review this list with your teen before disappointing dorm decisions are made.

1. Crown Jewels
There are no crowns in college (unless you decide to loosen a bottle cap with your teeth) and there are no jewels. Bummer.

2. Moats
Don't be fooled. Royal dorms are less than authentic as there are no moats on campus.

3. Ladies-in-Waiting
Heads up, college women—the only ladies-in-waiting are your roommates waiting for you to put on your mascara so you all can hit a frat party. Speed it up.

4. Royal Crests
Maybe your family's got lineage, but chances are your only crest is gonna be toothpaste.

5. Dungeons
You can call it a dungeon, but when push comes to shove, it's still only a basement. There, the only prisoners are the ones doing laundry.

6. Royal Suitors

Sure, spending your days roaming about the palace for royal suitors will increase your chances of getting a title, but that title is likely to be "unemployed." Rule your own monarchy and study.

• • • • • •

The Frugal Tourist

It's easy to get caught up in the moment and caught off guard by college touring expenses. Fortunately, there are many ways to cut costs. Touring nearby universities, regardless of student interest level, can help students identify campus preferences like school size before committing to costly travel. Bundling tours with other travel obligations (work, vacations, weddings) can minimize commuting and hotel costs. Utilize lodging that includes free breakfasts and frequent traveler perks.

5 College Tour Mistakes

1. Skipping the tour
2. Asking the guide her ACT scores
3. Using your cell phone
4. Arguing with your child
5. Not exploring beyond the tour

Consider letting your child visit and stay with a college friend. Discourage tours of schools that are financially impossible. Don't create the opportunity for disappointment and dollar drain if it really isn't an option. And last but not least, refrain from impulse purchases. Pricey "College U" fleece and logo'd water bottles seem necessary at the time, but if your child heads to a rival school, these items are headed for the thrift store.

● ● ● ● ● ●

MOTHER OF THE RIDE

One mom took college visit chaos and university road trips into her own hands and created a solution. Z. Kelly Queijo founded SmartCollegeVisit.com, a web site that makes planning college visits easier for college-bound teens and their families. Users can search for colleges, plan and book travel, and even calculate gas costs. Students can also track their visits and create a profile page to share with colleges. With over 500 tour videos, and articles on all things college, SmartCollegeVisit.com proves some moms really do drive the process.

● ● ● ● ● ●

Admission Anxiety

Parents and students often regard the college admissions office as some sort of Oz. A surreal, magical place that seems to hold the futures of high school seniors, this Oz intimidates naive visitors. Applicants study and visit and write to impress. Parents obsess and speculate. Some avoid contact when they have genuine questions, fearful they will be pegged as pesky, a notch against them on some imaginary list next to the receptionist's phone. Others call about nothing, illustrating their obsessive-compulsive tendencies or hope that contact will give them an edge. Ironically, admissions office professionals are not the untouchable people behind the curtain. Many are among the most understanding, cut-you-a-break kind of people you will ever meet.

Your Friendly Admissions Office

After interviewing admissions professionals from all over the country, I learned the last thing to be is fearful of is an admissions office. Here's why....

Admissions office professionals understand 17- and 18-year-old minds. They know their interests, problems, and quirks. They've seen it all and heard it all from students and parents. And every year, most of them sign back up and do it all over again. Admissions professionals emphasize that the college application process is not a faceless one. They become invested in the applicants, and while they don't get attached, it can be an emotional process as they face the ethical and practical dilemmas that surface in any selection process. They don't take admissions decisions lightly. They're excited for accepted students and feel badly for those they cannot accept.

Genuine Is Fine

If anyone has anything to fear, it is the dishonest applicant and parent. Admissions professionals value honesty. They are experts in this process and have an uncanny ability to detect inauthentic applications. They've seen slick submissions from the financially privileged, great but plagiarized essays, and they aren't impressed. They are impressed with a genuine application, an essay that's well written and not ghostwritten, and an applicant who shows interest in the college and them whenever their paths cross.

> ### 5 Do's for Parents
>
> 1. Let the applicant make the admissions office contact
> 2. Encourage the applicant to attend the college's high school visits
> 3. Insist the applicant fill out the applications
> 4. Encourage the applicant to research the school
> 5. Encourage the applicant to write a thank-you after every interview

Back Off

Sometimes you just have one question, and by the time your child gets home from school, the admissions office is closed. Too bad. Your student needs to drive this process and the admissions office will notice that. Do not phone them while using your best Valley Girl voice. Do not email pretending to be your child. They notice because frankly, the over 40 crowd isn't that good at pulling off the teen thing.

All Roads Lead to the Admissions Office

Students and parents sometimes forget that admissions office impressions are formed beyond the application and interview. College representatives who staff college fairs and attend high school visits are often the people involved in the selection process. Students should be engaging and prepared to take advantage of another opportunity for information gathering on both sides.

Show Interest

The admissions office notices when students show interest through college visits, high school visits with reps, calls, and alumni contact. They are impressed when interviewed students are knowledgeable about their college and ask thoughtful questions. Students should know the schools that interest them. Reviewing college websites and brochures before contact can lead to better interactions. Applicants should also use these opportunities to let representatives get to know them better. This is the time for students to share their interests, aspirations and accomplishments—it's not bragging if it's the truth.

No Gifts Please!

Do not send gifts. Gifts of food are still gifts. Grandma's baklava may be good, but it's also manipulative. If you're thinking of creative gift giving, don't. It's just plain wrong. No parent should ever dress up in costume and deliver a gift basket. (Yes, it has happened.) It won't give your kid an edge, and people will make fun of you.

No Call Backs

In the unfortunate event that your child is not accepted, do not call the admissions office. They already feel badly. Making a bad situation awkward will not change the decision.

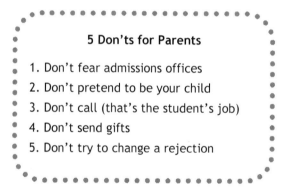

5 Don'ts for Parents

1. Don't fear admissions offices
2. Don't pretend to be your child
3. Don't call (that's the student's job)
4. Don't send gifts
5. Don't try to change a rejection

Images and Interviews

Interviews can be scary when your senior's idea of dressing up is wearing a t-shirt that isn't black. Interviews give universities a behavior sample of an applicant. Some parents hope their sample will be better than the glimpses they see at home. What if teen eye rolling is a reflex? Might a teen go all "know-it-all" on an interviewer and tell them how to restructure their tours? It's never that bad, but a neurotic parent has to find something to worry about.

Some institutions emphasize interviews and campus visits, believing that this contact reflects the student's interest level. Others, because of enrollment size or recognition of student financial and geographic limitations, do not emphasize or encourage interviewing. Either way, your senior can benefit by preparing for an interview. Below are instructions for applicants—not parents—that can help with interview preparation.

What to Wear

Teens should discuss interview attire with guidance counselors, friends, and college freshmen. They shouldn't stand out in any extreme during the interview. That means no three-piece suit or cocktail dress if everyone else is in jeans. No jeans if everyone is in khakis. Neatness and modesty count.

What to Ask

It's always best to have a few questions for an interviewer. Specific questions related to student interests or special programs illustrate the applicant's interest and that she has done her homework. Reviewing college brochures and websites before an interview can generate questions and refresh memories. Write down three to five questions you have about the college. This will help you avoid that "deer in the headlights" look when asked the dreaded question, "Is there anything you'd like to ask me?" At the same time, don't just ask a question for the sake of asking. Make it real. This is easier if you review college materials ahead of time.

What to Say

Re-read your essays, college application, and résumé before the interview. Be prepared to answer related questions—a good reason for you to be honest as you write your own essays! Be yourself. If you're so nervous that your hands are shaking, acknowledge it and move on. View this as your opportunity to show the college why you are the perfect candidate. Beyond the standardized test scores and GPA, what should they really know about you? One of the hardest things for many students is being comfortable talking about their accomplishments. Marketing yourself is not the same as bragging.

Promoting yourself is not the same as bragging.

Look for gaps in your résumé and transcript and determine if there are any critical points to discuss. Did a family move and transition to a new school create hurdles for you? Did you work to supplement family income at the expense of your GPA junior year? Write down three to five questions an interviewer might ask you and then answer them.

Indicate your specific interests in a school. If the only reason you can pull out is the climate and beautiful architecture, it becomes clear that you aren't committed to that school. Don't be afraid to talk about your interests even it's an obscure hobby. If you're passionate about paleobiology and have been speaking with one of the professors about research opportunities, bring that up to the interviewer. If you sat in on a class, visited the school twice and have been in touch with student groups, be sure to share that, too.

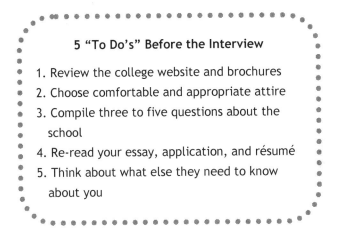

5 "To Do's" Before the Interview

1. Review the college website and brochures
2. Choose comfortable and appropriate attire
3. Compile three to five questions about the school
4. Re-read your essay, application, and résumé
5. Think about what else they need to know about you

What to Do

Don't assume they know your enthusiasm just because you showed up. There are plenty of seniors who are only sitting in that interview chair because their parents insisted. Be polite and engaging. Smile! Kindness and humor are contagious, but don't be a jokester. Most people can't pull off comedy and unless you're great at it, this isn't the place to try. Be comfortable making eye contact. It's difficult speaking with someone who avoids eye contact. Shyness may be the cause, but it can be misinterpreted as disinterest. Turn off your cell phone. I'm happy you've got unlimited texting, but it doesn't mean it's okay to text during an interview.

Say "Thank You"

Once back home, take time to thank your interviewer with a handwritten note or email. Make sure you've got the name and spelling right. Thank-you notes should mention your interview experience and subtly help the person remember you. Not all interviewers care about thank-you notes, but take a lesson from Mom—thank-you notes never hurt!

5: APPLY YOURSELF

No, you're not applying. It just feels that way. College applications are exhausting, even if you're only monitoring the situation. Barely recovered from those campus road trips, you're living in a land mine of applications and essays. True, these really aren't parental problems, but they can morph into them. When teens are overextended, anxious, procrastinating, or indifferent, it is a parental problem. Endless and intimidating paperwork combined with senior schedules and attitudes can be a challenge for family harmony. Inevitably, someone will tell someone else to "take a chill pill" and it won't help a bit. Take a deep breath, give good advice, and keep your student in the driver's seat.

The Dating Game

Yes, it's all about dates. And they're not all the same. Whether your child is applying early decision, early action, rolling admission, or regular decision, offer to help her sort out the deadlines and details of each.

5 Application Facts

1. Over-applying can burnout applicant
2. Over-applying can burn out finances
3. Attention to detail is critical
4. If teens don't like the school, they won't like applying
5. Kids who apply to please parents, panic when accepted

What's the best application option? It's hard to say. Applying early decision means getting applications in earlier and, if accepted, the process, chaos, and anxiety of applying is over in December. Many college experts believe that applying early decision may give an applicant an advantage, because many universities select a larger portion of applicants from this pool.

What's the catch? Early decision applicants are also less likely to receive financial support (although there's always an exception) and, because of the parameters of the early decision agreement, cannot explore alternative offers from other universities. Once a student receives early decision acceptance, she is obligated to withdraw her applications from all other schools. Early decision is a comfortable option if it is clear one school stands out above all others, and that financial negotiation is not necessary. Then, just in case, prepare to accept responsibility for full tuition.

• • • • • •

TOP TIP

If you want to compare competing financial aid offers from colleges, don't apply early decision.

Jane C. Hoffman, M.B.A., College Admissions Advisor

• • • • • •

I've always thought of early action and rolling admissions as "having your cake and eating it too." Receiving early acceptance without being locked into a decision can be anxiety-reducing for students and parents. It can give a student negotiating power and the opportunity to be a comparison shopper. As a parent, I think of this as a more humane way to play the game, but only if your child is organized enough to meet the deadlines. If she's the queen of procrastination, then regular decision is your friend because it equalizes the playing field—presumably, early responders don't have an advantage.

Honorable Mention

> Don't bombard colleges with additional recommendation letters.

Great recommendation letters are important for admissions success, so students should get this ball rolling early. Your senior needs letters from people who know her well, like her, and can convey that. Teachers from junior or senior year are often the best choices, because they can address the recent skill sets of the applicant; however, teachers who've only known a student for a few months may be at a loss to find enough to say. Your teen should supplement the writer's memory with her résumé and, if needed, a transcript. And don't bombard colleges with additional letters. An extra letter should be sent only if it offers a unique perspective to the application. If wait-listed, a student should send an additional recommendation letter to update an application and confirm continued interest.

Application time is hectic for popular teachers who write well. Remind your teen to send a note or a thank-you email to those who supported her in the college-bound process.

Sounds easy enough, right? It is—unless your child is a late or haphazard requester. Late requesters take their procrastination and wrap it around every aspect of the college application. These individuals will "get around to it" when it comes to securing the important recommendation letters. The late requester believes teachers can knock off a few dozen letters in a single night.

The haphazard requester puts no logical thought into the person she selects to write her letter. She may pick a "fun" teacher from a class she barely passed, a "cute" teacher all her friends are using, or a tough-as-nails English teacher who writes well but doesn't like her.

5 Tips for a Great Recommendation Letter

Advise your student to:

1. Give the writer plenty of time
2. Choose someone who likes you
3. Choose someone who writes well
4. Give the writer your résumé and transcript
5. Avoid bombarding the admissions office with extra letters

Truth or Consequences

Student success can be sabotaged by a misguided parent's behavior. Guidance counselors, admissions officers, and therapists see it all the time: parents doing high school homework, and writing college term papers, graduate school essays, and job résumés. If they could pass for 17 and slip into skinny jeans and an SAT or ACT testing site, these parents might take the tests, too. Sending the message that you are your child's personal assistant, or that you can do it better, is dangerous for your child and her college career.

Children's applications can be driven by parental desires. A teen who applies only to please (or shut up) a parent, probably spends more time praying she's rejected than completing a top-notch submission. One student applied to 100 colleges just to annoy his pushy parents who had insisted he apply to places they wanted but he hated. It worked; they were annoyed. But he also wasted a lot of time and cash in the process.

Another student was rejected for an incomplete application, or to be more exact, a parent's incomplete application. Unfortunately for the student, Dad accidentally put his own name on the application when he filled it out. Force of habit was the driving force behind that rejection. Admissions officers caught on when there were no supporting materials for Dad Doe. Tsk tsk! Ghostwriter Papa was probably kicking himself for not thinking ahead and naming son "Junior."

> Ghostwriting can kill an application.

* * * * * *

TOP TIP

I truly believe that students who take time to showcase themselves beyond their transcript have an edge during the decision-making process. While I was an admissions counselor, I spent more time considering the applicant who came for an interview, submitted a résumé or electronic work, and connected with me online. It's easier to picture a student at my school when I know them as a person.

Gil Rogers, Former Associate Director of Admissions,
Director of Marketing and Outreach at Zinch

* * * * * *

Essay 4-1-1

If you looked up "college essay" in a thesaurus, "frustration" and "hair pulling" would be somewhere nearby. Getting kids to write college essays can be like pulling teeth, except with tooth extractions, there are ways to numb the pain. Essay writing isn't fun for most writers or their nagging parents. But every year, colleges boast about record-breaking application numbers, so somehow these things do get written. Read on and learn how to nudge your student toward progress and essay success.

P.S. If you're feeling superior because your teen has taken the bull by the horns and is doing it all beautifully without your push or panache, we don't want to hear about it. Stop gloating and skip to Chapter 6.

The essay counts. While importance can differ greatly among schools, the essay is often one of the most valuable pieces of an applicant's portfolio. A good essay helps the reader understand the student; a great essay makes the reader want to meet her.

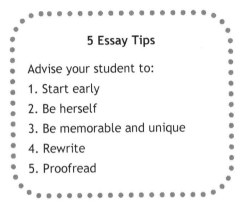

5 Essay Tips

Advise your student to:
1. Start early
2. Be herself
3. Be memorable and unique
4. Rewrite
5. Proofread

Good News, Bad News

Admissions professionals want the applicant to write the essay. Phew, that's good news because most parents haven't written an essay since the '80s. The bad news? You may have to light a fire under your senior to get the ball rolling. That's right, on the road of college applications, SAT and ACT anxiety is matched only by essay procrastination.

You are probably the normal parent of a normal, college-bound senior if you have dreamed or screamed about an essay. It's a touchy subject that touches many families. Procrastinating applicants frustrate parents; and over-controlling parents irritate seniors. Some parents go over the edge, breaking moral and ethical codes, writing essays and filling out applications because they believe it will stop the insanity. Ironically, this lying fuels the insanity and compounds the problems.

Ghostwriting Won't Fly

For the last 17 years, most of us have been shaking our heads at how different we are from our kids. They don't act like us or reason like us. And yet, some parents think they can write their senior's essay and no one will notice. A 40-plus voice is very different from an 18-year-old voice. Admissions officers don't expect the polish of a university professor or successful litigator. Like parental intuition, admissions office intuition is sharp. As a former admissions committee member, I witnessed the secrets behind the essay. You don't need a magnifying glass to find hidden messages like, "I can't spell to save my life and I don't care enough to spell check" or "You are just my safety school." And the biggest loser, "Somebody else wrote this for me." A fantastic essay written by someone else will not cover up a bad transcript or poor test scores.

* * * * * *

TOP TIP

Proofread your child's applications. Don't write the essays and over-edit applications—your child's voice must shine through. As much as you want to Thesaurus.com your child's essay, hold off; a college will instantly detect the voice of an over-eager 45-year-old!

Dr. Katherine Cohen, College Admissions Expert,
CEO and Founder of IvyWise and ApplyWise.com

* * * * * *

A Dozen Pointers

1. Consider Starting Early

Word counts count.

Some high school teachers and counselors suggest students look at essay questions during the summer prior to their senior year. While these won't necessarily be the same essay questions, getting a jumpstart on application theme review, personal reflection on accomplishments and aspirations, and brainstorming can help decrease the pressure when senior classes begin.

2. Follow Directions

A student shouldn't skim the essay question or ignore word counts. If the word requirement is 300–550, a 100- or 800-word response isn't wise. Beware of stories of unique essays that worked (the one-word response, the purple striped paper); they are often a gamble that can backfire.

3. Be Honest

A good essay is truthful, but it's not a therapy session. This is not the time to disclose uncomfortable information or to address sensitive subjects that may offend others. Choosing topics like drugs, sex, religion, and politics could be a touchy choice if not well crafted. Topics that tend to be overdone can bore some reviewers, despite their importance (e.g., death of a loved one, parental inspiration, national

Honesty is the best policy.

catastrophes). However, if these topics are truly important to the applicant, she should write with conviction.

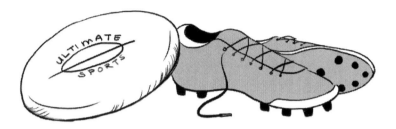

4. Be Memorable

Your teen should generate a positive and unique impression. If she is passionate about Frisbee® and has lobbied to make Ultimate a recognized sport in her school, she should include that. She may be tagged the Ultimate fanatic, but that tag may be what makes her more memorable than the other 200 applicants with the same GPA and standardized test profile. She might also be surprised to learn that the college rep plays on an Ultimate team.

5. Be Enthusiastic

Generic doesn't cut it. Cookie-cutter answers that can be plugged in to any application suggest a lack of interest. Colleges want to know a student will attend if offered admission.

6. Get Started

Procrastination and perfectionism are the enemies in essay completion. Encourage your student to sit down and write—even if it's just off the top of her head. Getting a few good sentences down can spark an entire essay.

● ● ● ● ● ●

TOP TIP

It's important for colleges to choose who will choose them, so
students must show their enthusiasm.

Deena Maerowitz, J.D., M.S.W,

Founder, Undergradadmit.com

● ● ● ● ● ●

7. Spell Check, Grammar Check, Fact Check

Using spell check doesn't eliminate the need for
proofreading. Grammatical errors can be spelled perfectly and
can be perfectly embarrassing. With today's spell check
programs, automatic features can also pose problems. One
student's typo and auto-correction made it look like he was
involved in recreational drug use. He mistyped "ultimatum"
and the computer gave him "opium." Fortunately, it made
someone laugh. Unfortunately, it was an admissions officer.

8. Read It Aloud

Sometimes by reading the essay aloud, a student can hear
her message more clearly. Reading the last sentence first will
show her if it has the power to grab the reader.

9. Review and Revise

Plan for computer
malfunctions.

Some senior English classes require
students to write a college essay for evaluation, revision, and
grading purposes. This can be a useful project, but for those

without this resource, a teacher or skilled adult can help. Students should choose someone who will be a good proofreader and sounding board. This adult should be willing to proofread and critique the essay for errors, content, and tone. A good essay usually requires revision, and some involve as many as five revisions.

Great coaches and tutors are only a phone call or computer click away. Research the options with your child.

10. Wait

If time permits, your student should postpone sending her application until at least one day after it is completed. This will give her another opportunity to rest and re-check.

11. Save

Computer and electrical malfunctions happen. (This is also why waiting until the night before a deadline to send an application is never a good idea.) Your teen should always save and print a copy of her essay and application. Having a hard copy on file can also be a helpful timesaver as additional school and scholarship applications are completed.

12. Send

Tah dah! She did it. Remind your teen that it gets easier, and each essay has the potential to either be modified or used as a springboard for another school's essay. Just beware—proofing is key to ensure that the essay and its characteristics match the targeted college!

> **5 Reasons Not to Proof Your Kid's Essay**
>
> 1. You often confuse "their" with "there"
> 2. You've never put much stock in the apostrophe
> 3. "It's" and "its"—it's all the same to you
> 4. You never got that "i before e" thing
> 5. You just had your eyes dilated

Let's Make a Deal

Proofreading can keep you in the loop. While some applicants welcome parental input, this is not the norm. Not every parent-child relationship is strengthened by this activity. If your teen runs screaming when you look over her shoulder, help her find a qualified person to assist. High school teachers, coaches, independent advisors, and friends can help guide students toward completing competitive applications.

* * * * * *

TOP TIP

Writing is hard. We take our words personally. Be very delicate in critiquing your kid's words. If that's hard for you, encourage him or her to forge a good working relationship with a favorite teacher.

Ned Johnson, President and Tutor-Geek,
PrepMatters , Inc., Co-Author of
Conquering the SAT: How Parents Can Help
Teens Overcome the Pressure and Succeed

* * * * * *

To Tell the Truth

Not every parent has seen writing samples from their high school student, so reading the college essay can be shocking. Some seniors write like English professors, proving parental involvement unnecessary and potentially harmful. Others' essays are so disjointed, you wonder if you should have stepped in long ago. Relax before you review and remember that the first draft is often just a springboard for a great essay.

Be advised; reading your senior's essay can make you feel like you walked in on a therapy session. Some teens self-disclose differently than their parents and it's not unusual for themes to be a little darker. Do not criticize, but gently suggest this might not be ready for submission.

> Proofreading your child's essay is a thankless job, but somebody's got to do it.

If you choose to be involved, be thick-skinned because the comments usually aren't pretty. I once pointed out a spelling error and got accused of being OCD. When unhappy with parents, teens often resort to diagnosing them with stigmatizing conditions. Stay strong.

Many parents are more detail-oriented in the college application process than their children. That may be because we're more mature, but we also don't have a calculus test, physics final, stack of applications, practices, rehearsals, and standardized testing looming over us. If we did, maybe we'd back off on proofreading too.

The Common App

Over 400 institutions participate in the Common Application. Fondly known as "The Common App," it can help students avoid repetition in the college application process, keep track of submissions, and focus on one essay. Participating schools are bound by the philosophy and ethics of the Common App—no favoritism for school-specific essays over the Common App essay. While the Common App was meant to be calmin', additional essay requirements are still commonplace in the world of college admissions. Hang in there; she'll be done before you know it.

＊ ＊ ＊ ＊ ＊ ＊

My Common App Essay

When I saw this essay question for the Common App, it got me thinking—"Indicate a person who has had a significant influence on you and describe that influence."

A parent should never write a child's essay, but she can write her own. Here's mine....

I should have known that someone who could influence my diet BEFORE we even met, would become a powerful force once he appeared. My college applicant has been influencing me ever since.

YEAR 1: This small being has single-handedly changed my sleep habits. I wake up at the littlest noise. I crave multiple naps—his and mine.

YEAR 2: I'm running much faster now. I can dive across the room in a split second to save him or something from him.

YEARS 3–4: I'm using a lot of one-syllable words, especially "no." It's not going over well.

YEARS 5–6: Soccer is now one of the most important activities in my life. I watch it in the pouring rain and freezing cold. Everyone gets a trophy but me.

YEARS 7–12: He begged me for a minivan and I caved. I have to admit it's working well, as I spend 95% of my time driving him around. There is also enough room to nap and transport a ficus tree.

YEAR 13: There's a detectable attitude shift. The child who idolized me is now rolling his eyes and contradicting me. The sweet little baby bear is a grizzly.

YEARS 14–15: Ya gotta love reliving high school. The homework. The social scene. The bad football games. I'm more anxious than he is.

YEAR 16: He got his driver's permit! The former minivan advocate now uses his free time and forensic skills to try to convince me that an SUV is a less embarrassing form of teen transportation.

YEARS 17–18: He's got his license, my car keys, and college applications to complete. My sleep is shot because I have one ear open for the garage door to go up, and the other one listening for college stories. My one eye is open for test scores and the other for deadlines. I'm exhausted but know it is temporary. Soon he will be in college. I'll have my car all to myself and I'll call him just to say how much I miss him. Right after my nap.

* * * * * *

6: GETTING IN AND CHECKING OUT

Stand back—it could get nasty. That wonderful feeling of relief your family's been experiencing since the college-bound student hit the "send" button is gone. The clock is ticking and the verdict looms. Panic is in the air and anxiety is running high. You'd run for the hills, but you can't look frazzled or concerned. It's your job to be supportive and upbeat. Some days are easier than others.

The Waiting Game

"It's not really great over here right now," my friend and MOS (Mom of Senior) warned. "Early decision letters come out this week and one of his friends already got a 'yes'. Now we're forbidden to even open the mailbox. He thinks we might discard the letter with a Food Mart circular."

I'd been there. My senior's mood swings made me consider medication—for myself. As notification time approaches, living with applicants can be impossible. High on anxiety, they live in fear that the sacred envelope might be buried in a catalog, thrown in the trash, or blown into a cornfield (and your house is on a cul-de-sac). To prevent mishaps and natural disasters, they change house rules and become the only one sanctioned to do mail runs. Parents of these applicants don't have to struggle with the urge to open the anticipated letter, because they can't get close enough to the mailbox to see if it's there.

In addition to postal anxiety, the waiting senior has been known to avoid peers who have received positive letters. Peers with coveted acceptances to his number one school cause excessive worry. ("How many spots can there be?") Those with rejections can be equally scary ("I'm probably next"). Quiet support works best this week, because nothing you say will give him the answer he wants—"You're in."

Senior theories about decision-letter timing are often wrong. When others' good news comes first, they're certain they're slated for rejection. You spend 90% of your time shooting down convoluted theories. There's often no rhyme or reason in sequencing. You can't predict the message based on the timing of decision letters. Acceptances don't reach everyone on the same day. Someone has to get the first acceptance letter. He will find little comfort in this. If he is fortunate and gets a very early acceptance, remind him to be kind and supportive to those who continue to wait.

Email acceptances introduced a new neurotic behavior—hovering over the "refresh" icon. It is the virtual replacement for mailbox guarding.

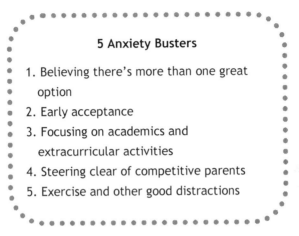

5 Anxiety Busters

1. Believing there's more than one great option
2. Early acceptance
3. Focusing on academics and extracurricular activities
4. Steering clear of competitive parents
5. Exercise and other good distractions

High Anxiety

Just the other day, you were sick of the college solicitations and now, when you are allowed, you scan the mail searching for special envelopes with familiar logos. Every good parent wants their child to be happy, so this is no picnic. The morning shows feature stories on cut-throat college competition. Rumors are flying and your head is spinning. National Merit® Scholars and future valedictorians can't even get into their safety schools. To cap it off, everywhere you turn, you're hit with the same question: "Where'd you get in?" Where'd you get in? You got in way over your head when you signed on for this project. But don't worry; things will calm down. Just a little more anxiety as you watch fellow parents beam over their child's acceptance. Big smile. Deep breath.

Special Delivery

Even the minimally inquisitive parent is tempted to hold THE envelope up to the light (steaming is illegal) or weigh it against some imaginary criteria. Has anyone ever proven that acceptance letters weigh more than rejections? Do email rejections come with smaller attachments? This isn't your Oscar moment. Let your teen open the envelope. (Unless he's asked you to intervene.) Hold the letter up to the light if you want to, but you'll see nothing. Not that I would know or anything....

Broadcast News

During the waiting week, tempers may fly and tears may flow, but when the acceptance letter arrives, the world stops and turns your child all "Stepford." The senior that you tiptoed around yesterday is now the nicest, giddiest version of himself you have ever seen. He gladly walks the dog, is kind to siblings and as chipper as a love-struck teen. Enjoy it. Take videos if you can, because this wonderful cheeriness will soon be replaced by the self-important, "I knew I would get in" attitude. Fortunately, parents are used to change and unpredictability. Here we go again....

• • • • • •

EARLY ATTITUDE

It happens right around the time you hear those voices telling you to fill out the FAFSA. Have you noticed everything unpleasant is linked to an acronym? Sure, the family's left SATs behind, but the winter's long and dreary. SAD (Seasonal Affective Disorder) doesn't help, although you can buy a light for that. January and February are difficult months for parents of smug college-bound kids because that's when EDA surfaces. Early Decision Attitude occurs after the month-long euphoria of getting in to the college of choice. It is characterized by a change in sleep and study habits (A LOT LESS!) and accompanied by the familiar phrase "RELAX,

I'm already in college." The symptoms of EDA are often exacerbated when the student sports university logo apparel. While EDA is usually normal, parents who let down their guard can be as surprised as their early-decision students. (Yes, acceptance letters are based on continued outstanding performance.). So, keep an eye open and the light on your senior. Better safe than sorry and sad.

• • • • • •

Disappointment

Not all letters bring the messages we want. Rejection doesn't feel good, and often parents feel worse than their seniors. It's much easier to help your child through the rejection experience if you've kept a balanced and logical approach to the college application process. Parents who have emphasized or encouraged the idea that there is only one perfect fit for their senior won't have an easy time. Seniors who have second and third choices they love are more resilient than those who are unable to picture themselves anywhere but one place.

● ● ● ● ● ●

TOP TIP

Don't focus on one school or get defeated when your child does not get in, as it adds unnecessary stress. (So visit the safety schools on your child's list and get excited about them!) If your child creates a balanced college list, (s)he will get into a "good fit" college where (s)he'll be successful and happy.

Dr. Katherine Cohen, College Admissions Expert,
CEO and Founder of IvyWise and ApplyWise.com

● ● ● ● ● ●

The majority of disappointed seniors quickly turn enthusiastic about another school. If I could say one thing to a devastated senior once he was ready to listen, it would be this: "I have never met a well adjusted adult who claimed a college rejection ruined his college experience or life success. Some have even claimed it to be a blessing in disguise."

Steven Spielberg applied to the University of Southern California's School of Theatre, Film and Television. He was denied. Twice. Decades later, he was awarded an honorary degree from USC and became a University trustee. Uncomfortable life experiences are slices of reality that teach us valuable lessons. Sometimes it takes awhile to know what they are. Spielberg's experience proves a rejection letter is meaningless when it comes to brilliance, talent, and where you land in life. That's good news. Life's successes are tied to one person, not one school.

❋ ❋ ❋ ❋ ❋ ❋

TOP TIP

As harsh as it sounds, most wait-listed kids don't end up getting admitted. At first, that seems awful, but instead of focusing on the negative, help your child reframe the experience. Your kid was too strong a candidate to be denied. If the applicant pool had been smaller or if the college had had more room in the incoming class, your child would have been admitted! Colleges can't admit all great applicants. Help your child move onward.

John Carpenter, Educational Consultant,
www.askjohnaboutcollege.com

❋ ❋ ❋ ❋ ❋ ❋

Waiting Room

Just when it seemed like everything was black or white, your child gets gray. Being wait-listed can be more stressful than being rejected, because there is no definite answer to act upon. Fortunately, there are actions that can help a wait-list candidate all the way around. Being in this position forces a senior to contemplate other colleges. This can help him realize that great options still exist. At the same time, the verdict isn't in. If your senior really wants to get off the wait list and in for real, this isn't the time to drop the ball.

Some wait-listed students immediately choose another option. The admissions office has no clue who is interested and who has moved on. Once wait-listed, the interested senior should keep an updated list of academic and extracurricular accomplishments to forward to the college in a single document before March. This can include academic awards, outstanding coursework performance, improved standardized test scores, and sports updates. This letter and relevant attachments (e.g., newspaper clippings) will provide the admissions office with confirmation that he is a strong candidate for admission who didn't "check out" in January with senioritis.

No matter what, the senior should send something to demonstrate continued interest, even if it is just an updated transcript or an additional letter of recommendation. This will put him in the "still interested" pile.

Alternatives

It's never too late to find alternatives. Be open-minded and think outside the box. Many students have found wonderful experiences in round-about ways, whether it be last-minute slots in interesting university programs, courses in the trades, or a gap year in an exciting location. Take a deep breath and encourage your senior to investigate some more.

● ● ● ● ● ●

STICKER SHOCK

It fell out of the most important letter of the year. A thin adhesive sticker tucked inside the anxiously awaited university acceptance letter.

"Mom, I got in!" my son exclaimed. "Now you can get off my back."

I might have cried, but I was too busy thanking a higher power for giving me my life back. The admissions office insisted I didn't owe them that phone call. Like proud parents everywhere, I took the highly coveted university decal mobile. Clinging to the rear window of our SUV, the victory sticker symbolized closure from a process I thought would never end. This would be the last and most expensive decal on the journey of parenthood. Soon the nest and the bank account would be empty.

"What will you do with your time now that you won't have to nag him to write essays and study SAT words?" my mother asked.

That's when it hit me...maybe I could offset college sticker shock by creating my own line of empty-nest bumper stickers. I was never a bumper sticker mom, but I've spent enough time on the road to notice the epidemic. Ever since they took baby on board, people have been taking their family business out for a test drive. For the put-it-out-there proud and bragging parent, car decals are a way of life. For some, they are the best invention since vanity plates. We know their children's names, sports, musical instruments, and grade point averages. If the university sticker is the end of an era, empty nesters will be in decal deprivation once their honor students secure bachelor's degrees.

"Let me get this straight—you feel obligated to create a line of midlife bumper stickers?" My husband wasn't convinced.

"That's right, there are creatures of habit out there with midlife messages to broadcast. I can't sit by and watch them drive off into the sunset of their lives in stickerless sedans, proclaiming absolutely nothing."

I showed him three samples.

For the midlife driver with night vision problems: "I brake for just about everything"

For the midlife driver with a little extra time: "I ♥ naps"

For the empty nester with senior moments: "I think my kid was an honor student"

"Those are very cute," he conceded, "but this sounds like a big commitment. I kind of thought you'd have some time for me once the kids were gone."

"Excellent point." I jotted down another one sure to generate profits that will cover four years of college.

For every woman with a needy spouse: "BIG baby on board"

** One of the winning essays of the
2010 Erma Bombeck Writing Competition*

● ● ● ● ● ●

Ridiculous Reasons

Few seniors know exactly what they want to be or where they want to be when they grow up. College is a time for exploration of options. Sometimes the rationale given for college choices seem illogical to the academically inspired parent. Some kids choose schools based on social factors, hobbies, and landscape. One mom confided that her son favored one school based upon an enjoyable lunch at a sub shop. In this case, a cold cut combo was inspiring.

Fortunately for him, it was a good school and a good fit. Still, it illustrates that crazy reasons don't exclude an excellent educational opportunity.

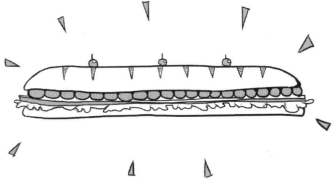

Guard Duty

When my son got his early-decision acceptance letter, I thought I could relax. But contrary to the popular senior belief, vacation hadn't started yet. There were five months of grades to go and a university that would not tolerate a GPA in a downward spiral. So I preached the need to keep grades high.

"Your admission can be revoked if your grades drop," I reminded him.

His eyes sparkled. "Precisely why I'm changing all my AP courses to my real interest—photography."

> Don't let your child check out too early.

My little Ansel Adams didn't realize that, while photography courses were exceptional and challenging, the application transcript was part of a contract. Changing classes, especially to ones that might be perceived as less rigorous, can void that contract/acceptance.

A novice would think you could hang up your haranguing ways once the acceptance letter arrives. But parental tasks have only shifted. Now you must make sure that student performance doesn't crash as senioritis soars. You can't blame a senior, really. Is there anything more ego-feeding than a piece of paper that tells you how special you are to have been chosen over thousands of incredible candidates?

Adolescent egocentrism is normal, but when paired with a college acceptance letter, it can quickly turn into into "I'm already in—why sweat the calc test?" The parental answer: "Because if your grades slip, your acceptance can go away!"

5 Parent Tips

1. Expect the "grades don't matter" attitude after acceptance
2. Keep an eye on school performance
3. Don't allow course changes without university approval
4. Talk about the consequences of irresponsible behavior
5. Ask a teacher or guidance counselor for support

That sticker may be on the SUV, but the deal can be broken by bad grades, newfound laziness, and irresponsible behavior. (Senior pranks and parties can result in suspension, arrest, and revocation of college acceptance.) Guidance counselors and favorite teachers are usually skilled at issuing senior reality checks. They've heard every student suggestion and excuse. Versed in prevention, they are also loaded with real-life disasters and retractions that can hit home. Let the storytelling of others help your student stay on task, but keep your eyes open, too. There'll be plenty of time for relaxation next year.

7: CHEERS AND TEARS

Whoa! The ceremony that once seemed so far away is right around the corner. You've held your breath through testing, bitten your tongue during touring, and covered your ears to temper the tantrums. Now you're relieved and wondering if you'd wished it away too quickly. Don't worry; after the cheers and tears, you'll be too busy to second-guess yourself. There are so many more hoops to jump.

Pomp and Circumstance

After you're done sweating the big stuff and the small stuff of college admission, there's a good chance you'll still be sweating. That's right. High school officials are notorious for scheduling graduation in venues that can't keep anyone cool. Wear light and cool clothing, so the only thing you'll be swelling with is pride. Regardless of the temperature, you'll

> "Pomp and Circumstance" has a universal way of erasing bad memories.

always love this day. "Pomp and Circumstance" has a universal way of erasing bad memories. This is the way it should be—a year of cramming and curfews ends with smiles and video footage. Parents and college-bound teens bask in the glow of a high school diploma and college acceptance letter. Homes once flooded with paperwork and doubt, are now filled with cake, punch, and well wishers.

Then it happens. The happy graduate comes bounding over to you with an armload of checks and gift cards. She sees dollar signs (normal). You see thank you notes and another opportunity to bicker about her need to start writing (pretty normal). Yes, it would have been nice to relax until it was time to bond at Bed Bath & Beyond®, but you might need to do one last etiquette drill before that moment. Try this:

Her: Can I use your car this weekend? I have THREE graduation parties.

You: Sure, right after you write a few essays, I mean thank you notes.

---

5 Characteristics of the New Graduate

1. Focuses on graduation parties
2. Rarely home
3. Begs for later curfew
4. Delights in dining out without you for every meal
5. Uses "but I'm leaving for college" as universal excuse

Senior Circuit

Who wouldn't be excited? The pressure's off and vacation has officially begun.

Happy families are hosting lots of parties and graduates are getting all the attention. Emotions run high. Grads hug each other like they're being deployed and decide this summer they will do nothing but say farewell to their peers—even ones they really never liked. There is little time for family, chores, or packing for college. Fortunately, you don't need a search party to track down your graduate—just a party invitation—because that's the only activity that seems to be scheduled two weeks before, during, and after graduation. Caution: newfound freedom combined with parties and teen attitude can spell disaster. Be on the lookout. There are plenty of laws and rules to enforce.

> It's hard to be upset about an empty nest when your baby bird's a vulture.

Pompous Circumstances

The "attitude" of the graduate is well documented. Somewhere on the heels of graduation comes the "you're being ridiculous" attitude, which is very different from the "you can't tell me what to do; I'm in college" threat that appears after they return home for winter break. Post-graduation exuberance and gratitude have evaporated, and rudeness and lack of appreciation can creep in. A psychologist colleague reminded me this was normal. A teen's rude behavior and disrespectful ways were just attempts to separate, to make the ultimate separation (college) less painful for the child and the parent. Maybe my colleague was right; it's hard to be upset about an empty nest when your baby bird's a vulture. That's not to say that disrespectful behavior is acceptable. Just understand that there could be friction as college gets closer.

> The graduate's priorities seem to be sleep and hanging out with her friends.

In between this normal struggle for independence there are still opportunities to create positive memories. You just have to work harder to find them, because the graduate's priorities seem to be sleep and hanging out with her friends. Try to schedule family time and consider including friends to maximize the likelihood she'll show. Look for ways to make quality time out of necessary chores like shopping, packing, organizing, and list making. Then be happy you've raised a social child.

Note: If you want to maximize last-minute time with your child, encourage her to pick a school where move-in day is later than all of her friends'. When they clear out, she'll be so bored, she'll beg for your attention.

• • • • • •

EXTRACTING WISDOM

Many families check off another important milestone right before the college launch: oral surgery. This pre-college dental rite of passage just might be the universe's way of giving parents one final dose of feeling really needed before the dorm drive-by. Wisdom teeth extraction packs every aspect of parenting into a 24-hour period: chauffeuring (someone's got to drive the sedated teen to and from the procedure), worrying, pain control, comforting, hovering, issuing restrictions, and providing food. A successful experience involves giving it up to a great oral surgeon and focusing on ice. Ice packs. Ice cream. Armed with a milk shake, any parent can be a teen's hero. Once the patient is resting comfortably, a parent is left to ponder.

How did those pesky molars get their name?

If these teeth are so wise, why do they grow the wrong way?

And isn't extracting wisdom from a college-bound student a bad idea?

Maybe, but it's time to let go of worrying. A milk shake might help.

● ● ● ● ● ●

College Credit

Forget the colored pencils and 25-cent glue stick specials; this back-to-school shopping expedition is different, and your credit card's taking the hit. It's expensive. It's complicated. And it's kind of fun. An extra-long twin bed sheet and Febreze® may be the staples for dorm life, but there's so much more to purchase and pack! From linens to electronics, clothing to comforters, it can be a logistical nightmare no matter how you lug it.

In the pre-send-off frenzy, parents and teens are prone to overbuy. Wouldn't ten tubes of toothpaste be better than one? What if they don't sell Pop-Tarts® in Wisconsin? At the same time, some items may be substantially cheaper when purchased at home. Stock up on these things, but remember, she's not going on safari. Future supplies can be delivered on

> Don't short-sheet your teen. Dorm beds require EXTRA-long sheets.

parents' weekends or obtained during holiday breaks. Note: Most chain drugstores have a prescription database. Your student can likely refill her prescriptions away from home.

Beware of dorm restrictions. Most universities have strict housing policies prohibiting candles, certain kinds of lighting, cooking appliances (except microwaves), furniture, and pets. Overzealous and uninformed shopping could mean you'll be toting some of the purchases back home. And who's going to help you unload the car?

If packing space is an issue, consider ordering items online and schedule campus delivery or local pick-up. (Bed Bath & Beyond has a popular program.) Or consider my younger son's favorite approach: place a sleeping bag (friends might visit), all linens, comforters, pillows, and winter coats in a Space Bag®. Vacuum until you create the thinnest, heaviest piece of plastic you've ever seen. You might need someone to help carry it, but that's rarely a problem on dorm drop-off day. You'll be able to see out the car rearview mirror and drive through a carwash with the windows open and

everything inside will still be dry—except you and the electronics.

Wheeled duffle bags work well for packing and moving, and will fit easily under a dorm bed. Most universities also have well organized move-in days, characterized by plenty of energetic and cheerful upperclassmen and lots of carts with wheels. In most cases, there's no need to worry about breaking your back or teen valuables.

5 Things They'll Forget to Pack

1. First aid kit
2. Medicines
3. Thermometer
4. Flashlight
5. Scissors

Child Care

There's a good chance before your college-bound student has even packed, you will be asked to demonstrate how much you care. Letters arrive with plenty of suggestions on how you can do this. For a chunk of change, companies will keep reminding your student how much she is loved by sending her gift baskets on Halloween, Valentine's Day, and any time an exam rolls around. Yes, you care, but does she care about a few cocoa packets, herbal tea, and a candy bar? Maybe. If not, building your own care packages can be cheaper and better received. Tip: An Amazon Prime^{SM} membership gives families unlimited fast shipping on amazon.com, including free two-day shipping on eligible purchases (from food to music) for a fee that's less than a pricey care package.

• • • • • •

Bed Bath & Beyond Embarrassing: Dorm Decorating Tips from My Son

When *USA Today* College posted advice for dorm decorating that would make students "feel at home," I had to take a peek. Inexpensive tips from paint color to flameless candles, and lace trim to glass vessels for nail polish, transformed drab dorms into shabby chic cool. While I was ready to move in, it was apparent these beautiful solutions wouldn't make my college-bound kid feel at home. Have you seen his room? Let's just say he won't be using accent pillows until there's a relationship and a commitment pushing him into it. Here's the tips he'd give for preventing homesickness and creating a room that feels like the one he's leaving behind.

1. Eliminate the middle man and forget the hangers. Why create an extra step? Place all clothing on the floor where it can be easily accessed for wearing and laundering.

2. Mountain Dew® cans, when creatively stacked, can double as dorm sculptures.

3. Leave all academic paperwork strewn around the room. It will remind you of your primary mission—learning. When nagged by neat roommates, emphasize that some people have time to clean; others make studying a priority.

4. Forget about under-bed storage boxes. While clever, they only slow down your ability to kick stuff under there.

5. Don't be too hard on yourself; it's not a mess if you can still find your electronics.

• • • • • •

The Freshman 15

Step on the scale yourself before you start whining about campus vending machines, cafeteria food, and the Freshman 15. If you've been busy creating your kid's special recipes and revisiting her favorite restaurants before she ships off to college, there's a good chance this summer you'll suffer from the Freshman Parent 15. Parental pounds are packed on as you squeeze every ounce of family time out of every meal. This farewell food tour results in a carb assault on parents with midlife (there, I said it) metabolism. Proceed with caution or buy stretch pants.

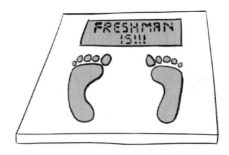

* * * * * *

PACKING: COLLEGES GO TO THE DOGS

Just when I thought my biggest hurdle was getting my college-bound teen to leave his Xbox® at home, InsideCollege.com posted a list of universities that allow pets in their dormitories. Now if my son picks the right pet-friendly college, he'll have the opportunity to be distracted by co-eds and canines. And I'll have the opportunity to worry about whether he's eating well AND feeding the Jack Russell. While this could give him the opportunity to use "the dog ate my homework" excuse for four more years, I doubt the pet benefits outweigh the inconvenience and potential hazards.

Then there are the schools that introduce pet options you've never considered. One accepts rodents and sugar gliders. Sugar gliders? I know what rodents are. I used them to threaten my kids when they left food in the basement: "Clean this mess up or we'll have mice." Thanks to Google®, I now know what sugar gliders are and I'm pretty sure these small gliding possums would like stray french fries too. Maybe a liberal pet policy is a cleaning option for the very messy. All I know is that the Xbox isn't looking so bad right now.

* * * * * *

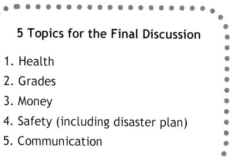

5 Topics for the Final Discussion

1. Health
2. Grades
3. Money
4. Safety (including disaster plan)
5. Communication

The Dorm Drive

Sure you've been talking all summer, but this is no time to stop. Your new college student should be reminded of the rules and expectations involving grades, finances, and high-risk behaviors. Initiating this dialog isn't always met with a warm response, but you've got skills. Some of the best kid conversations have happened in the car, so the ride to college can be perfect for this if you have parent-child privacy and a brief "put down your cell phone" agreement. On the other hand, if baby brother's in the back seat, find another time and place.

Be careful not to send your child off with unrealistic dreams of college as a flawless experience. It can be wonderful, but it is often difficult. Studying and relationship-building don't tend to be stress-free activities. Fortunately, most universities have strong student support infrastructures. From counseling centers to learning centers, campuses are filled with programs and people devoted to enhancing teen adjustment and well being. Encourage her to ask for help when she needs it.

As you pull away from your child and campus, it will hardly seem real. Things are going to be different. For a moment, you wonder if you can really handle the separation. Then it hits you—by the time you drive home alone, it'll be time to turn around for Parents Weekend.

● ● ● ● ● ●

TOP TIP

Advice for students: Treat college like a job, even if a part-time job. You have so much freedom, so much more time in college. Organize yourself by devoting, say, 9–12 to class time and 1–4 to coursework and studying. Do that Monday through Friday and rare will be the need for a late night or, worse yet, all-nighters that can derail you.

Ned Johnson, President and Tutor-Geek,
PrepMatters , Inc., Co-Author of
Conquering the SAT: How Parents Can Help
Teens Overcome the Pressure and Succeed

● ● ● ● ● ●

Worrying

Here's the crazy part. You spend years working with your child so she will get into college and then you cry because she's going. In the end, you will worry about all sorts of things. Some border on ridiculous. Is withdrawal imminent if the dining hall doesn't serve mac and cheese? Will she really make an 8 a.m. class if you aren't banging on the bedroom door? Who will remind her the day before an exam? Will cleaning ever cross her mind or is pest control inevitable?

* * * * * *

TOP TIP

It seems that some students and parents have unrealistic expectations of the college experience. While college is a wonderful, life-changing experience, it can be difficult, painful, and certainly expensive. College is a part of life...not all of life, and not necessarily the "best years of your life." In fact, I tell people that if college does turn out to be the best years of life, then for most people the best years of their lives are over at 22. That's depressing.

Sidonia M. Dalby, Associate Director,
Office of Admission, Smith College

* * * * * *

Some concerns are legitimate (including pest control, but we won't go there). A million worst-case scenarios play out in your mind. The detail is so vivid, it's as if the incidents have already happened. And if you totally trust your kid, there's still no peace, because you've got to worry about everyone else's kids. You draft a safety checklist longer than a pharmaceutical insert.

And then there are the little nagging concerns that few parents talk about. Will the child I saw every day for 18 years forget to call? Will the relationship change forever? If you are lucky, the answer to these questions will be "yes"—in a good way. A college student who has successfully adapted and is academically challenged sometimes forgets to phone home. And in the end, as your college student establishes independence and becomes a responsible adult, your relationship should change. Be proud and take heart that she doesn't have to wait in line to use a dorm phone to call you. Thanks to technology, family contact is easy. Don't worry; you'll be hearing from her. This adventure is just beginning....

The Disappearing Act

Okay, so maybe she's not calling much. Don't panic yet. ET phoned home faster than my younger son. Great social lives and plenty of studying often result in missing-in-action status. There is no correlation between how strong your relationship is and how much she calls. Don't nag long-distance. Unless there's a safety concern, wait a little bit longer and then phone or text her.

When it seems like it's been forever since she's called, here's a hint that just might get communication rolling. I once got three text messages in one minute from my college freshman after texting him the following: "At Costco^{SM}. Anything you need when we drive up Parents Weekend?"

> Don't nag long-distance.

* * * * * *

THE OVERBEARING PARENT WISH LIST

Face it—college students have tight budgets. And they need to study, not worry about what to get you the next time your birthday or a holiday rolls around. Here are a few ideas for your student that are sure to make any helicopter parent or tiger mom happy.

1. Ask your student to sign you up for Skype and keep the account open at all times. This way you can monitor her study habits and the company she keeps.

2. Suggest she skip a few lattés and buy you an unlimited texting plan. Checking in with her six times a day will help decrease your anxiety.

3. Have her create a Facebook account for you and friend you. Have her friends friend you, too. Now when your college student can't reach you, you can start a phone tree.

4. Ask your student to introduce you to her professors on LinkedIn. You only want what's best for her, and that anthropology prof needs a wake up call anyway.

5. Ask for an air mattress so you'll have a place to crash at the dorm. Who needs a Marriott®? You've got some catching up to do.

* * * * * *

The Changing Nest

Whether your nest is empty or just slimmed down a bit, your life will change. When my younger son left for college, one question was hurled at me daily. "What do you do with all of the extra time?" Now, people aren't stupid, which is why that question baffles me. Isn't it obvious? I'm doing what most parents do when they ship kids off to college or launch them into the real world; I'm trying to operate electronics on my own. The changing nest is a time of continuous discovery and insight. You will identify the color of her bedroom carpet, because you can see the floor again. You will find more free space on your DVR and fewer pizza boxes on garbage day. You will discover there is one less person weighing in on your wardrobe choices and a lot less laundry. You're still the only one who manages to unload the dishwasher, but even that's less frequent. And after your first grocery run, it will become embarrassingly clear exactly who you were really buying those corn chips for.

It's a little sad, but very exciting to watch your teen move forward. Will you ever stop worrying? Probably not, but there's light at the end of the anxiety tunnel. As the nest empties, there's a lot less time to worry—you're too busy trying to reprogram the cable remote and kicking yourself for thinking you could work the Blu-ray®. Don't worry—winter break's just around the corner....

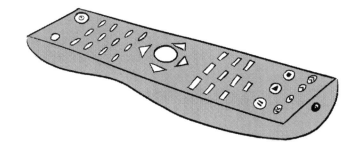

MEMO

To: University Faculty and Staff
From: Office of Admissions
Date: September 1st
Re: Tiger Cub on Campus

Be advised that during Freshman Move-In Day, a tiger cub was spotted on campus. While this is a harmless creature, faculty should proceed with caution, as tiger cubs are often closely followed by Tiger Moms. Should you see a Tiger Mom, please refrain from mentioning anything that resembles fun and extracurricular activities. The term "Social Mixers" can trigger attacks, and "Spring Break" once resulted in the hospitalization of an R.A.

While we do not anticipate any serious campus threat, it is always wise to be vigilant in the university setting. Jungle animal parents can pose hidden dangers to your well being and teaching efficacy. Other types of jungle animal problem parents are listed below.

- **Ostrich Dad:** Prefers to stick head in the sand or run away when confronted with a problem. Phone him and you'll get nowhere.

- **Giraffe Mom:** Has an amazing capacity to stick her neck out and nose in where it shouldn't be. She's got you on speed dial.

- **Hippopotamus Dad:** Looks cool and harmless but one of the most aggressive of jungle animals. He acts like your friend but he's SO not.

All faculty and staff are encouraged to travel in pairs until these parents calm down.

EPILOGUE: CONTRADICTIONS

"I can't wait to see you, too," he said.

Finally, my 18-year-old college freshman had become the young adult son of my dreams. His every-other-day phone calls proved he was now a conversational, mature adult. And he missed me!

His return was one of the best days of my life. When your college kid comes home for the first time and he's all-around happy, a parent basks in the glow. Grades were good, social life "amazing," and there wasn't a trace of anxiety. Phew.

Our typically non-demonstrative kid hugged me and his father. We jumped into a rare family dinner. There were no complaints or food critiques. He initiated a non-mandatory discussion and asked for our opinions. We all laughed. He got along with his brother. Our first day was like television in the '50s. It would be hard to let him go back.

"Could I have your car later tonight?"

Of course he wanted to see his high school friends. Everyone was home for winter break. I gladly turned over my keys.

After a 105-day hiatus, I slept with one eye open again. It was uncomfortable but familiar, a small price to pay for an independent, responsible adult child.

I woke up happy and exhausted. Caffeine would help.

I headed for the coffee maker and got a dose of reality. After months on a meal plan and ramen noodles, a college student let loose in a kitchen with a fully stocked pantry is dangerous. A mac and cheese encrusted pan was still on the stove, half a loaf of garlic bread was stuck to a baking sheet, and a frozen lava cake had been forgotten in the microwave. I'm pretty sure this is what a cooking show looks like when the clean-up crew bails.

> You spend three and a half months anticipating their return home; and about three and half hours into into it, you're counting down the days until they go back.

I marched upstairs and opened the door to chaos. My film major was apparently minoring in set design. In less than 24 hours, he had transformed a spotless bedroom into a location for *Animal House* or any Judd Apatow movie. The new champagne linen comforter was now orange thanks to a Doritos® mishap. And it smelled like the Lakers had popped by for a post-game visit before showering.

"Get up RIGHT NOW and clean my kitchen," I demanded in a voice I hadn't used since August. "Is there a reason you decided to have a 2 a.m. *Iron Chef* moment and not pick up after yourself? It's like an explosion down there."

He rolled out from under the covers, piles of clean and dirty clothes (the duffle bag had been emptied), and electronic devices surrounding him. "RELAX, I'll do it when I get up." He rolled back under the debris.

That's when I realized college changes kids, but maybe not that much. Fortunately, once he cleaned up, my kitchen was better than I'd left it—spotless except for a plate of homemade fudge. He took care of everything and whipped up a little treat once he got up, which was … right around dinner time—a little late, but just in time for dessert.

APPENDIX A: COLLEGE-BOUND PET PEEVES

5 Parent Pet Peeves

1. Student indecision
2. Student procrastination
3. Information overload
4. SAT/ACT anxiety
5. Guidance counselor college biases

5 Student Pet Peeves

1. Non-stop parent talk about colleges
2. Parental nagging about applications
3. Standardized testing
4. Being forced to apply to a school
5. Touring an undesirable campus

5 Guidance Counselor Pet Peeves

1. Parents doing their child's work
2. Parents who force their child to apply to a school
3. Senior procrastination
4. College coaches who breathe down their necks
5. Students who think acceptance equals vacation

5 Admissions Officer Pet Peeves

1. Flooding them with excessive materials
2. Parents who contact them on their child's behalf
3. Parents who call or write pretending to be their child

4. Parents who show up at the office with gifts
5. Parents who call after rejection
   (everyone feels badly; nothing can be changed)

APPENDIX B: TEN MONEY-SAVING TIPS

A good education comes in all price ranges; so does a college search.

1. Standardized test prep doesn't have to be expensive. Do some research and find strong programs online (actstudent.org or collegeboard.org) and in the community.

2. Borrow college-related books and materials from graduating seniors.

3. Take advantage of informal college visits early in your child's high school career by pairing tours with vacations and family visits.

4. Application fees add up. Don't encourage your child to over-apply. Ask colleges for application fee waivers if there is financial need.

5. Use virtual tours to preview campuses and narrow down college visits.

6. Visit local colleges to determine your child's campus preferences before you head out on more expensive long-distance college tours.

7. Use your airline and hotel travel points to help fund the college tour.

8. Avoid the impulse to buy campus logo items at every stop.

9. If the family's college budget doesn't include long-distance travel, create a college perimeter. Identify the maximum distance between home and college that will work for your student. Then examine colleges inside that perimeter.

10. People value what they pay for. Have your child save some money for college.

APPENDIX C: COLLEGE-BOUND FAVORITES

My Favorite Big College Book

Fiske Guide to Colleges 2012. Sourcebooks, Inc., 2011

My Favorite "What Parents Really Want to Know (or not)" Book

The Big Book of Colleges 2012. College Prowler, 2011

My Favorite Books to Keep You Grounded

College Unranked: Ending the College Admissions Frenzy. Lloyd Thacker (Ed.). Cambridge, MA: Harvard University Press, 2007

Colleges That Change Lives: 40 Schools That Will Change the Way You Think About Colleges. Loren Pope. Penguin, 2006

My Favorite "Can't Stop Thinking About the Ivies" Book

What Colleges Don't Tell You (And Other Parents Don't Want You to Know): 272 Secrets for Getting Your Kid into the Top Schools. Elizabeth Wissner-Gross. Penguin, 2006

My Favorite Standardized Test Resources

Conquering the SAT: How Parents Can Help Teens Overcome the Pressure and Succeed. Ned Johnson and Emily Warner Eskelsen, New York: Palgrave Macmillian, 2007

Cracking the SAT, 2012 Edition. Adam Robinson and John Katzman. Princeton Review, 2011

Kaplan SAT 2012: Strategies, Practice, and Review. Kaplan Publishing, 2011

The Official SAT Study Guide. The College Board, Henry Holt & Company, 2009

The Real ACT Prep Guide. 3rd Edition. Peterson's, 2011

My Favorite Online Resources

College Admissions and Applications

- ◆ The Common Application for Undergraduate College Admission:
  www.commonapp.org

- ◆ My College Calendar:
  www.mycollegecalendar.org

- ◆ National Association for College Admission Counseling:
  www.nacacnet.org

- Zinch:
  www.Zinch.com

College Visits and Virtual Tours

- CampusTours:
  www.campustours.com

- College Prowler:
  www.CollegeProwler.com

- Peterson's:
  www.petersons.com

- Smart College Visit:
  www.SmartCollegeVisit.com

- Unigo:
  www.Unigo.com

- YOUniversitytv:
  www.YOUniversitytv.com

Testing and Test Prep

- ACT:
  www.act.org

- The College Board:
  www.collegeboard.com

- Educational Testing Service:
  www.ets.org

- Kaplan:
  www.kaplan.com

- National Association for College Admission Counseling:
  www.nacacnet.org

- The Princeton Review:
  www.princetonreview.com

Scholarships

- CollegeXpress:
  www.collegexpress.com

- Fastweb:
  www.fastweb.com

- Free Application for Federal Student Aid:
  www.fafsa.ed.gov

- National Merit Scholarship Corporation:
  www.nationalmerit.org

- Scholarships.com:
  www.scholarships.com

- Scholarships360:
  www.scholarships360.org

- Student Aid on the Web:
  www.studentaid.ed.gov

COLLEGE-BOUND SHOUT-OUT

A special shout-out to those who answered my questions and told me their stories, including the Baldwin, Bracken, Breslof, Schwartz, and Ulanowicz families (we did it!), the Bennett family (you're almost there!), Fox Chapel Area School District faculty and administration, John Baxter, Akil Bello, Dan Berk, Hunter Berk, Ron Berk, Jeannie Borin, Mike Boylan, Kathy Caprino, Sarah Caron, John Carpenter, Donna Cavanagh, Eric Clark, Will Clower, Jenn Cohen, Katherine Cohen, Karen Connor, Sidonia Dalby, Tara Decomo, Michael Deegan, Evvy Diamond, Ivy Eisenberg, DeDe Fink, Judy Foxman, Kim Hodges, Emma Hoffbauer, Greg Hoffbauer, Jane C. Hoffman, Ned Johnson, Suzanne Kay-Pittman, Cindy Kichler, Myra Landau, Jill Langue, Dan Lawler, Mike Lopata, George Lynes, Deena Maerowitz, Doug Martin, Jane Mather, Mike McDermott, Timothy McLister, Erica Miller, Eric Monheim, Dave Mouldon, Claire Nold-Glaser, Lynn O'Shaughnessy, Joan Pfeffer, Priscilla Pilon, Z. Kelly Queijo, Christopher Chan Roberson, Perry Robinson, Gil Rogers, Dan Rosenfeld, Janet Rosier, Barbara Sams, Patti Schram, Suzanne Shaffer, Randi Sigal, Debbie Stier, Kim Thomas, Shane Torchiara, Marie Trudeau, Charlene Weted, Kelly White, and Betsy Woolf.

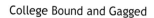

College Bound and Gagged

ABOUT THE AUTHOR

Nancy Berk, Ph.D. is a clinical psychologist, award-winning humorist, stand-up comic, and author. A frequent contributor to *Chicken Soup for the Soul*, she blogs for *The Huffington Post*, *USA Today* College, and *MORE Magazine*. Author of *Secrets of a Bar Mitzvah Mom* (2005), Nancy has been spotlighted in the *New York Times* and interviewed by the *Wall Street Journal*, CNN, MSN, and national magazines. One of the 2010 winners of the Erma Bombeck Writing Competition, she has appeared on television and radio, and hosts two podcasts: Whine at 9 and College Mom Minute. Nancy and her husband Ron are the proud parents of a college graduate and a college freshman. Check out her College Bound Blog on DrNancyBerk.com.

Made in the USA
San Bernardino, CA
19 December 2017